Finance in Brief

Six Key Concepts for Healthcare Leaders

Kenneth Kaufman

ACHE MANAGEMENT SERIES

Health Administration Press – Chicago, Illinois

Finance in Brief

Six Key Concepts for
Healthcare Leaders

Your board, staff, or clients may also benefit from this book's insight. For more information on quantity discounts, contact the Health Administration Press marketing manager at 312/424-9470.

Library of Congress Cataloging-in-Publication Data

Kaufman, Kenneth (Kenneth V.)
    Finance in brief: six key concepts for healthcare leaders/Kenneth Kaufman.
        p. cm.
    Includes bibliographical references.
    ISBN 1-56793-132-4 (alk. paper)
    1. Health services administrators. 2. Health facilities—Business management. 3. Health facilities—Finance. I. Title
    RA971.3 .K383 2000
    362.1'068—dc21   00-038313
                                                                        CIP

The paper used in this publication meets the minimum requirements of American National Standards for Information Sciences—Permanence of Paper for Printed Library Materials, ANSI z39.48–1984. ∞ ™

Health Administration Press
A division of the Foundation of
    the American College of
    Healthcare Executives
One North Franklin Street, Suite 1700
Chicago, IL 60606-3491
312/424-2800

Contents

Introduction

Why this book?

This book provides healthcare leaders and board members with an approachable primer on what is often considered a daunting subject—corporate finance.

Intended to help the wary "over the hump," it introduces six key principles critical to the effective financial management of all healthcare organizations: the capital management cycle, financial planning, creditworthiness, risk, capital allocation, and cost management. With a basic understanding of these principles, healthcare leaders will be equipped with a common language and approach to strategic decision making.

The need for this book is more pressing than ever. Healthcare has become a highly competitive business. To ensure survival, a healthcare organization's strategic mission must be supported by financially sound practices and a business plan that generates a positive bottom line. Once the province only of *Fortune* 500 companies, the language of corporate finance now must be understood by all individuals at the decision-making table in healthcare organizations nationwide.

Hence, this book is geared to leaders, senior managers, and trustees of all types of healthcare organizations, including hospitals (not-for-profit and for-profit), integrated delivery systems, networks, and long-term care, behavioral health, ambulatory care, home care, and other healthcare facilities. Formal financial training is not required; a receptive mind is required.

This book has been written in as user-friendly a way as possible. One note: Readers may need to read the chapter on risk (Concept Four) a bit more slowly than the other chapters. The extra time will be well worth it, however, because the chapter provides concise information on analytical techniques that will be critical to future financial decision making in a difficult healthcare environment.

What's in the book?

Organized in a question-and-answer format, the book has six chapters, each covering a basic principle of corporate finance.

Concept One, "'Round and 'Round in the Circle Game: Managing the Capital Cycle," describes why healthcare leaders need to worry about corporate finance and introduces the capital management cycle. It covers the elements of capital structure and describes who should be responsible for capital structure decisions. It also describes the characteristics of financially successful organizations.

Concept Two, "Follow the Yellow Brick Road: Financial Planning in the New Healthcare Environment," describes the financial planning process and the components of a high-quality financial plan. It takes readers through key steps of the process, including estimating capital requirements, determining capital sources, and determining the level of profitability required to close the capital shortfall. It also describes the techniques leaders can use to test the reasonableness of their projections and enhance the effective implementation of the financial plan.

Concept Three, "What's My Line? Analyzing and Boosting Creditworthiness," describes creditworthiness and why it is important to healthcare organizations. It outlines factors influencing access to capital in the current healthcare environment and the key determinants of creditworthiness as defined by the rating agencies. The chapter also provides the key ratios that should be used to analyze creditworthiness and describes how to perform a financial credit analysis.

Concept Four, "Hazards Ahead: Estimating, Taking, and Managing Risk," describes the difference between risk and uncertainty and the importance of both concepts to the healthcare decision-making process. It describes risk sources and the reduction of risk through diversification, and provides practical information on ways to visualize risk and uncertainty. It also provides information on the use of simulation to analyze uncertainty and on methods organization leaders and managers can use to evaluate healthcare projects, given uncertainty. Finally, the chapter provides guidance on putting the approach into practice.

Concept Five, "Spending the Dough: Allocating Capital," covers the capital allocation process and the characteristics of a best practices process. It describes who should be responsible for the process, strategies to ensure its successful implementation, and how to define the capital constraint. It also describes specific goals of project analysis and the first steps involved in the capital allocation process. It provides basic information on quantitative techniques that can be used to analyze a potential investment, including net present value analysis. Finally, the chapter covers methods for ranking and selecting projects.

Concept Six, "Towing the Line: Strategic Cost Management," describes a leadership approach that enables a healthcare organization to achieve the lowest possible costs consistent with delivering excellent quality care and customer service. The chapter covers who is responsible for this approach called strategic cost management, the approach's divergence from traditional cost reduction efforts, and ways to get started with its organization-wide integration and implementation. The chapter also provides information on the involvement of managers, clinicians, and staff in strategic cost management through interdisciplinary task forces, and the operation of such teams. Finally, the chapter describes the key ingredients for success with strategic cost management and the outcomes the approach can achieve.

A selected bibliography guides readers to relevant literature. Although the list of publications is by no means complete, it can serve as a starting point for additional information.

Acknowledgments

A book like this is a significant undertaking and it requires both inspiration and a collaborative spirit. Many individuals helped with both. First, thanks to Sam Savage and Michael Rindler for preparing chapters 4 and 6, respectively. Sam and Michael's work and thoughtfulness shine through in these two excellent chapters. The staff of Health Administration Press originally suggested this book with an eye to communicating critical financial concepts to a wide and diverse audience. Their suggestions have led to improved accessibility of the material without sacrificing accuracy or rigor. Nancy Gorham Haiman served as consultant and editor to the project. The book is immeasurably better for Nancy's efforts.

My colleagues at Kaufman, Hall & Associates contributed much to the book. I would especially like to recognize my partners of many years, Mark Hall, Therese Wareham, and Jason Sussman. I could not ask to work with more intelligent or more creative professionals, and many of the ideas contained herein originated with and were developed by Mark, Terri, and Jason.

My father, Felix Kaufman, is chairman of the finance committee for the Hospital for Joint Diseases in New York City. We have spent countless hours discussing the critical financial issues facing hospitals and thinking about ways to make those issues more accessible to hospital managers and board members. This book was greatly influenced by my father's ideas, his observations, and his keen intellect.

And, lastly, thank you to my daughters Rebecca and Sara and to my wife Barbara. Projects like this are made considerably better by a loving and supportive family. I am pleased to report that my family is all that and much more.

—Kenneth Kaufman

CONCEPT ONE

'ROUND AND 'ROUND IN THE CIRCLE GAME: MANAGING THE CAPITAL CYCLE

THERE ONCE WAS a lord of a castle. He lived in the Land of Three Rivers. His castle was a nice, comfortable one and the surrounding lands produced food aplenty for the lord and his people. In spite of prosperity, however, the lord hungered for additional lands. He annexed many fiefdoms within a very short period of time, some peaceably, some not. Most of the fiefdoms were poor and needed the lord's help for food and know-how about developing their lands. "No problem," thought the lord. "Within a year or two, the fiefdoms will be able to feed and fend for themselves and return goods to the Land of Three Rivers." Meanwhile, the lord developed the home castle and sent knights to conquer new lands.

As the lord expanded his empire, several of the new fiefdoms started to run out of food. They simply could not get up to speed as quickly as the lord expected. Unable to feed their own people, they certainly could not return food to the lord's castle to help feed others. Other fiefdoms followed suit. Within a year, the lord's empire had crumbled. He sold off the fiefdoms in faraway lands. Unable to feed his own people, the lord put his castle up for sale and moved away from the Land of Three Rivers in disgrace.

Sound familiar? This medieval rendition of Allegheny Health Education and Research Foundation's (AHERF) plight in 1998 illustrates the consequences associated with not understanding the "circle game" involved with the capital cycle. This game balances business strategies with financial ability. When played properly, it results in solid financial performance; when played poorly, it results in inadequate financial performance or worse. AHERF stumbled because its plan was built on the assumption that each acquired

I

hospital or entity could be made profitable within a short period of time. When a number of the hospitals performed poorly for multiple years, requiring a continued infusion of cash for operations, the pyramid built by AHERF's chief architect came tumbling down. Why? Going 'round and 'round in the circle game requires effective leadership comfortable in "playing the game," "talking the talk," and "walking the walk." Understanding the application of corporate finance principles is key. So is the proper management of the capital cycle. Quite simply, these were absent in the Land of Three Rivers.

Why do leaders and trustees of healthcare organizations need to worry about the principles of corporate finance?

Leaders of healthcare organizations need to know more than a little about finance to effectively manage their organizations. CEOs of *Fortune* 500 companies like General Electric and Microsoft certainly rely on corporate finance principles to manage the strategic and financial risk of their organizations. Why should things be different in the healthcare field?

In fact, increasing competition, declining reimbursement, and increasing regulation and complexity require healthcare leaders to be well versed in finance. They no longer can afford to treat finance as a stepchild. "Minor" decisions in the financial arena do not exist. All decisions have major implications for the organization's success and even, perhaps, survival. Once the domain of an organization's finance department, an understanding of corporate finance principles is now the responsibility of the organization's entire management team.

Healthcare boards of trustees must also possess an understanding of these principles. Being a trustee today simply demands a higher level of financial knowledge to ensure a common language in board rooms as decisions are made about whether to make an acquisition or invest in a clinical center, for example. Hospitals and other healthcare organizations nationwide are learning from the AHERF bankruptcy (see Sidebar 1-1). Board members now must demonstrate the ability to balance organizational values with solid financial practices.

SIDEBAR 1-1. Lessons Learned from AHERF Bankruptcy

L. Edward Bryant, a partner with Chicago's Gardner, Carton & Douglas, points to the following governance lessons from the AHERF bankruptcy:

- Too little formal director education;
- Board chair and CEO leadership was too entrenched;
- Over-reliance on the executive committee;
- Regular delegation of decisions to the board chair and CEO;
- Governance emphasized civic honor, social activity, and fundraising more than fiduciary responsibility;
- Too much paper was delivered too late with too little time for full deliberation of issues;
- Too little attention to alternative courses of action on proposals;
- Inadequate board involvement in formulating corporate strategic plans and setting priorities; and
- Too many "off balance sheet" transactions without adequate explanation.

Source: Reprinted from *Trustee*, vol. 52, no. 8, by permission, September 1999, copyright 1999, by Health Forum, Inc.

What is the capital management cycle?

The capital management cycle or strategic capital cycle is the circular path involved in managing the flow of capital from the development of strategic plans that require funding through financial implementation of selected strategic options and back to the planning process. The capital cycle includes three essential components that are both reinforcing and interrelated:

- A continuous *financial planning* process that is based on goals formulated in a strategic plan;

- A *capital structure* that is appropriate to the organization's current competitive and strategic position; and
- A *capital allocation* process that permits the organization to prioritize capital spending decisions in a manner that will improve the services provided while protecting long-term financial capacity.

Figure 1-1 illustrates the cycle. Managing the capital cycle starts and ends with the financial plan. This stage of the cycle is covered in Concept Two; capital allocation, the final component of the cycle, is covered in Concept Five. A description of capital structure appears later in this chapter.

Why is capital cycle management important to my healthcare organization?

Management of the capital cycle is absolutely essential to the positive financial performance of healthcare organizations. Senior leaders must understand how to achieve "best practices" cycle management and the technical and mathematical relationships between cycle components. Success or failure with one component affects success or failure in other parts of the cycle.

For example, without thorough financial planning, your organization will not know whether it is making the best use of available resources funded and allocated through the capital structure and capital allocation processes. Similarly, without access to required debt and equity capital ensured through the capital structure, an organization's strategic competitive plan is "dead on arrival." Faced with competitive pressures, organizations may be tempted to leapfrog over cycle steps, moving directly from the strategic planning process to implementation of strategic options, for example. However, the long-term financial success of complex healthcare delivery organizations depends on the development and maintenance of the financial plan with the careful and deliberate allocation of capital.

To succeed in a competitive environment, the capital cycle must be competently managed. This ensures that the organization is positioned to deliver

FIGURE 1-1.   The Capital Management Cycle

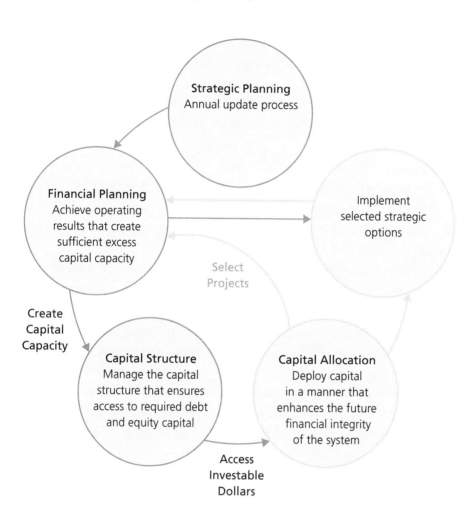

Source: Kaufman, Hall & Associates. Used with permission.

capital resources when and where they are needed to achieve strategic objectives. It also enables an organization to expand and renew capital capacity. Clearly, the long-term success of any organization depends on its ability to make capital investment decisions that will eventually add to and enhance its future capital capacity.

What is capital structure?

Capital structure is the combination of debt and equity that funds an organization's strategic plan. All healthcare organizations, whether for-profit or not-for-profit, must raise capital to buy the assets required to meet their strategic objectives. Capital comes in many forms, but, when obtained from external sources, generally is classified as either debt capital or equity capital. Internal sources of capital include operating cash flow (income, depreciation, and amortization), nonoperating cash flow (earnings and investments), and divestiture of marginal assets.

A broader view of capital structure considers such issues as the amount and type of debt and equity, cash, creditworthiness, and the legal requirements and obligations associated with outstanding debt. A description of two of these issues follows.

In the area of creditworthiness, the management of a healthcare organization's credit position is an essential component in the successful management of the capital cycle. Improved creditworthiness provides positive momentum to all strategic plans; deteriorating credit has the opposite effect. Throughout the 1980s and the early 1990s, most hospitals were accustomed to relatively easy credit and, for most of that period, low-cost debt. As a result, organizational creditworthiness was not a priority concern. With the AHERF bankruptcy, however, credit standards have tightened. Bond rating downgrades are outpacing upgrades, and bond insurance for healthcare debt has become more difficult and expensive to obtain (for more information on creditworthiness, see Concept Three).

On the topic of debt and equity, most healthcare leaders struggle with the basic question, "Is there an optimal mix of debt and equity financing, and, if so, what is it?" The mix depends on how much risk the leadership team wants to handle (see Concept Four). Those responsible for making capital structure decisions must ensure that the financing mix is consistent with the organization's strategic objectives. They also must determine how much debt can be reasonably included in the capital structure, and how much free cash will be available for reinvestment in the organization. Once the debt and equity mix decision is made, the next question becomes, "Given a specified level of debt, what's the right mix of short-term and long-term debt?" Leaders also need to address issues that will have an effect on access to and the cost of capital. These include the relationship of fixed-to-variable-rate debt, interest rates, amortization and maturity of existing and future debt, the flexibility of legal documents associated with existing debt, and the use of synthetic and derivative investment instruments in managing both interest rate risk and overall capital structure.

Capital structure forms a bridge between an organization's financial plan and capital allocation in the capital cycle. Proper management of the capital structure ensures access to required debt and equity capital and ensures a necessary consistency between competitive intent and the capital structure in place.

Who is responsible for managing an organization's capital structure?

Capital structure should be centrally assigned so that decision making and implementation are coordinated. Capital structure leadership must be driven by a knowledgeable senior management team that is chaired by the organization's CFO. The CFO and team must have technical financial skills and a coherent approach to capital structure. High-quality investment banking, legal, and consulting assistance is usually required as well.

What are the control points of healthcare financial management?

Healthcare financial leaders coordinate four variables throughout the capital management cycle: cash, profitability, debt, and capital spending. Figure 1-2 describes these points of control and their relative relationships. Based on its current financial position and external operating environment, each healthcare organization has an optimal "solution set" for these variables. This solution set is the preferred quantitative outcome between and among the points of control. Solving for the solution set through algebraic calculations is not required of senior management. Rather, the management team

FIGURE 1-2. Points of Control of Healthcare Financial Management

The "points of control" and their relative relationships are as follows:

- Cash: How much "free cash" should be on the balance sheet? Remember, creditworthiness is highly dependent upon liquidity, and cash is a direct source of capital, especially in the not-for-profit environment.
- Profitability: Profitability must be sufficient to support the required amount of debt capacity and ensure appropriate liquidity. The appropriate level of debt and cash will determine long-term profitability requirements.
- Debt: Not too much, as everyone knows, but not too little—a concept that is not sufficiently understood.
- Capital spending: How much is too much? How much is too little? The answers obviously relate to how profitable the organization is and the appropriate mix of debt and cash. A reminder: how an organization allocates its capital spending dollars can be more important than the absolute number of dollars spent.

Source: Kaufman, Hall & Associates. Used with permission.

must ensure that such quantification is accomplished, that the results and interrelationships between variables are well understood by the team and board members, and that the financial performance of the organization is safely managed within identified constraints.

What are the characteristics of financially successful organizations?

Financially successful organizations share four essential characteristics:

1. They recognize the need for and importance of financial leadership. The board and senior management team are accountable for managing the organization in a way that ensures attainment of financial goals and objectives on a consistent basis.

2. They understand that financial leadership is possible only through acquiring the necessary financial knowledge. In many organizations, a strong continuing education process is necessary to teach and reinforce critical corporate finance skills.

3. They commit to a "best practices" understanding of the techniques that guide the financial management of the organization. The CEO works in close partnership with the CFO, the chairperson of the board, and the chairperson of the finance committee to ensure that organizational decision making is guided by corporate-style financial planning and capital allocation processes.

4. They have a liberal dose of the "right attitude," which enables them to respond quickly and appropriately to a rapidly changing environment. For example, the popular press recently reported that some hospitals were surprised by the reimbursement effect of the Balanced Budget Act (BBA) of 1997. However, other hospitals with the right attitude reported that the expected effects of the BBA were anticipated and measured months prior to implementation and that the corrective actions needed to protect the bottom line were taken immediately.

How much finance do healthcare leaders need to know? More than they needed to know 15 years ago, or 10 years ago, or even 5 years ago. Clearly, to go 'round and 'round successfully in the healthcare circle game, they need to know more finance than ever before.

CONCEPT TWO

Follow the Yellow Brick Road: Financial Planning in the New Healthcare Environment

To FIND THE Wizard in the Land of Oz, Dorothy and her friends simply followed the yellow brick road. One path. A fork here or there, but nothing too troublesome. One big decision ... to proceed or not.

If only the healthcare world were similarly simple. It used to be. Hospitals were pretty much guaranteed a tomorrow. Schooled in the social service aspect of healthcare delivery, administrators made decisions largely based on intuition, trial and error, and, if fortunate enough, experience.

Few healthcare executives need to be told that their world is a changed one, now characterized by continuous transformations. Rapidly developing communication and technological advances have created an environment in which options, choices, and uncertainty abound. Experience, intuition, and trial and error no longer suffice as reliable executive decision-making tools. Why? The cost of making an error is just too high.

What is financial planning and why is it important to my healthcare organization?

Because survival is no longer a guaranteed option, wizard seeking is decidedly a different process. The new process involves the methodical and thoughtful integration of qualitative and quantitative thinking. Called "financial planning," this process is now key to an organization's survival *and* success. It involves deciding today what should be done in the future. A continuous process, financial planning includes establishing goals, objectives, policies, procedures, methods, and rules necessary to achieve the organization's purposes (Nowicki 1999).

A solid financial plan provides the backbone for a healthcare organization, and

- Links the organization's strategic mission and vision to measurable financial objectives;
- Helps an organization determine whether strategies are financially possible given the organization's capabilities;
- Describes future financial risk in quantitative terms, considers alternative scenarios, and specifies sensible reactions to expected or unexpected changes; and
- Enables the organization to react quickly and flexibly in a dynamic and complex marketplace.

Financial planning is the bridge between strategies and actions (see Figure 2-1).

Who is responsible for financial planning?

The healthcare literature is full of often-conflicting statements about who is responsible for the mission, vision, and planning in a healthcare organization. Some indicate that both strategic planning and financial planning are the province of the board of directors (Cleverley 1992, 180; Berger 1999). Others describe the CEO as taking the lead, with the board of directors serving as a strategic partner (Larson 1999). In reality, some boards establish mission, vision, and plans; others approve statements and plans developed by the CEO working with them and key colleagues.

We believe that the chief executive officer (CEO) is responsible for establishing a financial "vision." The vision sets forth what the organization wishes to accomplish given its healthcare mission. It includes concrete financial goals and objectives. The CEO must ensure that he or she has the financial training and experience necessary to establish the organization's long-term financial direction. For many, this means acquiring new skills and a working familiarity with analytical tools to remain at the helm.

FIGURE 2-1.   Financial Planning: The Bridge Between Strategies and Actions

Both the CEO and CFO must participate fully in financial planning. So too must senior managers, middle managers, and clinical staff leaders who are responsible for decision making and plan implementation. Although the CEO and his or her management team are responsible for ground-level financial decisions, members of the board of trustees must have a level of financial knowledge that will enable them to participate in and support decisions, as necessary, in the current challenging healthcare environment.

How does the financial plan relate to the organization's strategic plan?

An organization's *strategic plan* focuses both on external market needs and how best to meet those needs with the organization's resources. Strategic planning comes *before* financial planning. It involves trying to forecast marketplace changes such as demographics, payer mix, and reimbursement, and the effect such changes will have on the organization. The strategic plan tries to prepare the organization to use changes to the organization's best advantage (Sidebar 2-1).

Mission and vision statements provide the foundation for a strategic plan. From these flow a set of critical goals or objectives that will enable the organization to meet its mission. Next, the plan defines the initiatives — the programs, services, or activities desired during the plan period. The

---

SIDEBAR 2-1. Strategic Planning in Healthcare Organizations

Emerging from the corporate world, strategic planning was not well known in healthcare prior to the mid 1980s. By the mid 1990s, the process still had a very limited time horizon in most healthcare organizations. In fact, 61 percent of the provider organizations surveyed by Ernst & Young in 1996 did strategic planning with time horizons of less than three years (Ernst & Young 1996). Ten percent didn't even have a strategic plan.

    Garry D. Bruton of the University of Tulsa and colleagues propose that the lack of consideration of contextual issues has limited the success of hospital planning in the past. Such issues include ownership, size, and financial performance (Bruton, Oviatt, and Kallas-Bruton 1995).

---

financial plan assesses the feasibility of these initiatives. William O. Cleverley (1992, 205) of Ohio State University describes:

> The financial plan should not be developed in isolation from the strategic planning, nor should the strategic plan be developed in isolation from the financial plan. Both plans need to be developed together, reflecting in that context their individual requirements and assumptions. A strategic plan is not valid if it is not financially feasible, and a financial plan is of little value if it does not reflect the strategic decisions reached by management and the board.

A financial plan has a long time horizon—generally five years. It quantitatively identifies the profitability and liquidity requirements of the organization and establishes the organization's ability to acquire capital funds through debt or equity (Griffith 1999). It addresses the issues of funding and financing required to meet the organization's strategic objectives.

The financial plan supports the strategic plan by answering seven critical questions:

1. What are the organization's strategic capital requirements?
2. How much cash should the organization have on hand?

SIDEBAR 2-2. Components of a Strategic Plan

A strategic plan consists of
- A mission statement
- A vision statement
- An analysis of the organization's strengths and weaknesses
- Goals to eliminate weaknesses and capitalize on strengths
- Specific strategies and action plans to achieve goals
- Definition of critical success factors
- Financial planning for necessary resources
- Timetable
- Performance evaluation process for the plan

---

3. How much debt can the organization afford?
4. What short-term and long-term profitability targets are necessary to resolve any shortfalls?
5. What level of operating change is required to meet the profitability targets?
6. Where will the capital be obtained in the short and long term?
7. What transactions are required to obtain the necessary capital?

The financial plan provides the financial framework for achieving the strategic goals. Sidebar 2-2 describes the components of a strategic plan. Elements of a good financial plan are discussed later in this chapter.

The critical relationship between strategy and financial capability is illustrated in Figure 2-2. The organization's financial capability lies along the x axis; the organization's strategic financial requirements lie along the y axis. The "corridor of control" represents a balance between the two—in effect, an acceptable equilibrium situation. Over the long haul, every organization strives to achieve an appropriate balance between what it *needs* or *wants* to spend and what the organization actually *can* spend. If an organization falls above the corridor of control in the area labeled "short-term concern," its financial need or strategic appetite exceeds its financial capability. This

FIGURE 2-2.   Financial Planning and the Critical Relationship Between Strategy
and Financial Capability

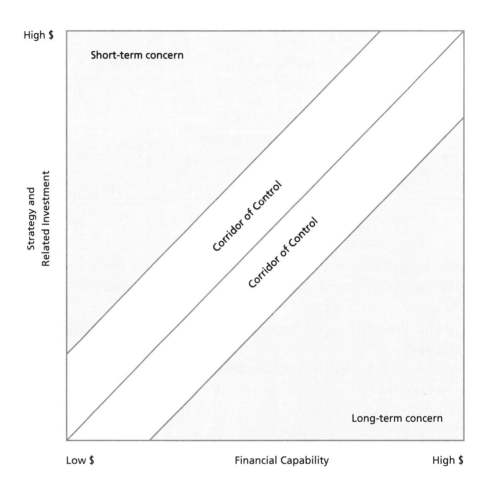

Source: Kaufman, Hall & Associates. Used with permission.

signals the need for management intervention to bring the organization back into the corridor of control.

For example, an organization that decides to merge with another organization frequently does so because it understands that its position in the need to spend/can spend chart has fallen within the short-term concern area. Instead of getting better (i.e., moving toward the corridor of control), the situation is getting worse and moving further up to the left. Eventually, an organization could move so far to the left that no number of operating changes could bring about its return to equilibrium.

An organization whose position appears *below* the corridor of control in the long-term concern area typically has a fair amount of money, but lacks a strategic plan outlining how to grow and spend that money. Its strategic financial requirements may be fairly low because of a conservative board and management or other factors. Such an organization generally is at risk of losing market share because it is not investing sufficient capital in plant and overall strategies while its competitors are doing so. Problems created by this approach manifest themselves more slowly than problems in the short-term concerns arena.

What is included in a good financial plan?

A sophisticated financial plan for a healthcare organization includes the following:

- Financial projections. Developed from accurate, well-maintained databases, these are capable of interactive, real-time analysis.
- Financial goals. These are flexible and easy to recalculate to allow for changes in the marketplace and strategic investment requirements.
- Capital expenditure requirements. Covering a five-year period, these include hard-dollar (projects and technology) and soft dollar (investments in physician networks and other integration initiatives) requirements.
- Debt capacity and cash requirements. These provide the "sources" side of the financial planning equation.
- An analysis of capital position. This compares the uses and sources of funds to identify any capital surplus or shortfall.
- Profitability calculations. These indicate the level of profitability that will close the capital shortfall and stabilize the organization.

Each portion of the plan is critical to obtaining the whole picture of an organization's financial health.

What is the first step of the financial planning process?

How do we start the process of developing a sophisticated financial plan? The first step is to measure, compare, and assess the organization's current financial performance and competitive status. To successfully plan for the future, you must have an accurate picture of current performance.

A credit analysis allows the organization to compare its recent financial performance to relevant national standards. It provides key indicators of financial strength and weakness and a benchmark of past and current creditworthiness. Organizations generally compare key indicators with Standard & Poor's, Moody's, or Fitch IBCA's ratings for other organizations in selected bond rating categories. For example, a hospital with an "A–" bond rating from Standard and Poor's (S&P) would compare itself to other medical centers with an "A–" S&P rating. The agencies publish rating data for not-for-profit hospitals and health systems on an annual basis.

Table 2-1 provides key ratios for freestanding hospitals and single-state healthcare systems in 1998. These ratios are defined in Concept Three. Key observations should be drawn based on the comparison with national data. For example, statements might include: "hospital has a relatively stable liquidity position," "profitability and operating cash show a downward trend," and "average age of plant is high." A full description of how to analyze your organization's creditworthiness appears in Concept Three. This step is critical to the success of future financial planning.

What are the next steps of the financial planning process?

The next step in the process is to define the financial and capital requirements necessary to ensure the organization's creditworthiness (i.e., profitability). This involves basic algebra. *Uses* of capital or the capital requirements appear on the left side of the equation. They include:

- Estimated capital requirements;
- Funding required to maintain minimum cash position; and
- Principal payments on debt.

**TABLE 2-1. Freestanding Hospital and Single State Healthcare Systems
Healthcare Medians by Rating Category, 1998: Selected Data***

	All Ratings	Aa	A	Baa	Below Baa
Distribution of Healthcare Ratings[†]	100%	11%	45%	36%	8%
Median Sample Size	303	35	142	114	12
Key Ratios					
Operating margin	2.2%	3.1%	2.6%	1.3%	0.5%
Excess margin	4.9%	7.7%	6.2%	3.3%	1.9%
Operating cash flow margin	10.3%	11.0%	10.8%	9.7%	8.4%
Return on assets	4.2%	5.3%	4.8%	2.9%	1.7%
Annual debt service coverage (x)	3.67	7.23	4.40	2.82	2.02
Maximum annual debt service coverage (x)	3.53	5.38	4.07	2.90	1.84
Current ratio (x)	2.0	1.8	2.1	2.0	1.5
Cash on hand (days)	154.6	255.2	200.5	100.2	39.9
Cushion ratio (x)	11.2	20.6	12.8	6.9	1.8
Cash-to-debt	98.7%	183.6%	115.4%	64.8%	22.4%
Accounts receivable (days)	64.2	66.6	64.0	64.2	59.2
Average payment period (days)	65.1	70.0	63.2	63.9	70.4
Debt-to-capitalization	37.7%	28.7%	35.4%	45.5%	63.1%
Debt-to-cash flow (x)	3.60	2.64	3.29	4.55	6.18
Average age of plant (years)	8.7	8.0	8.5	9.6	9.8

*Statistics are based on a sample size of 303 hospitals, excluding multistate hospital systems.
†Distribution encompasses all non-insured ratings as of 8/16/99, rather than the median sample.
Source: Moody's Investors Service. 1999. *Not-for-Profit Health Care: 1999 Outlook and Medians.* New York: Moody's Investors Service. Used with permission.

Sources of capital appear on the right side of the equation. They include:

- Unrestricted cash; and
- Net available debt capacity.

The solution variable is the level of profitability necessary to balance the uses/sources equation (see Figure 2-3 for a sample equation).

FIGURE 2-3. Capital Position Analysis, 2000–2004 (in Thousands)

Uses (2000–2004)	
Estimated Capital Requirements	$150,000
Funding of Minimum Cash Position (185.9 days operating expenses in 2004)	$216,202
Principal Payments on Existing Debt Structure (2000) and Proposed Debt Structure (2001–2004)	$20,400
Total Capital Uses	*$386,602*

Sources (1999)	
Unrestricted Cash 1999	$162,697
Net Available Debt Capacity	$0
Bond Related Construction Funds	$15,000
Total Capital Sources	*$177,697*

Estimated Capital Shortfall	*$208,905*

Source: Kaufman, Hall & Associates. Used with permission.

SIDEBAR 2-3   Calculating Annual Financial Requirements

An organization's annual financial requirements can be calculated as follows:

> (1) Annual capital expenditures
> + (2) Changes in working capital
> + (3) Actual principal payments
> + (4) Incremental expansion of debt capacity*
> + (5) Increases in cash on the balance sheet
> _____
> (6) Total annual financial requirements.

The first three requirements enable an organization to maintain "survival-level" financial performance. The fourth and fifth requirements enable an organization to perform competitively. Increased cash allows healthcare organizations to respond to the changing healthcare environment and preserve creditworthiness.

*See Sidebar 2-4 for a definition of debt capacity.
Source: Kaufman, Hall & Associates. Used with permission.

The journey to Oz begins with a single step, involving a reliable definition of financial requirements in year one (see Sidebar 2-3). Subsequent years must be as carefully defined so that the organization can reach its longer-term goals and objectives.

Answers to the next questions will guide readers through the process of developing and solving the financial planning equation.

How do we estimate capital requirements? How much should we be investing?

These questions are sources of endless confusion for many hospital executives and boards. They involve identifying the first variable (capital requirements) on the left side of the algebraic equation. To remain competitive, organizations must establish an appropriate level of investment in their facilities and clinical programs. The organization's strategic capital

---

SIDEBAR 2-4. Debt Capacity Defined

"Debt capacity" is the amount of debt an organization is capable of supporting. This figure must expand each year if the organization wants to
remain financially competitive. The ability to incur additional debt makes
the organization more responsive to its market and more resilient to expected and unexpected changes.

   For example, a hospital with a debt capacity of $50 million and out-
standing debt of $40 million has a net debt capacity of $10 million. If the
hospital's strategic plans calls for the $20 million purchase of physician
practices and ambulatory clinics in year five of the plan, the financial plan
should describe the incremental amount of debt capacity that must be
added to the balance sheet every year to raise the extra $10 million for
the purchases.

Source: Kaufman, Hall & Associates. Used with permission.

---

requirements should be outlined and based on objectives outlined in the
strategic plan for each of the plan years. Competitive information obtained
through national rating services (see age of plant information, for example,
in Table 2-1) can be useful for checking purposes. Armed with strategic information, your organization can develop a chart outlining capital expenditure requirements for the plan period.

   Next, your organization needs to determine the organization's total capital shortfall. *Capital shortfall* is the summation of capital uses less the summation of capital sources.

How do we determine other capital uses on the left side of the equation?

Other capital requirements or uses appearing on the left side of the financial planning equation include the funding required to maintain a minimum
cash position (days cash cushion on hand) and principal payments on debt
through the plan period.

Principal payments on debt can be determined based on the existing amortization schedules. The amount of minimum *cash reserves* is a major issue for many healthcare organizations. How much cash is enough cash? How much is needed to compete in a rapidly changing healthcare environment? Again, key competitive data from credit agencies can provide a starting place. One method of determining the minimum level of cash reserves is to use a days-cash-on-hand target. Another method uses the cushion ratio (cash and marketable securities plus board-designated funds divided by annual debt service). Competitive information on both cash on hand and cushion ratios can be found in rating agency data (see Table 2-1).

The target cash reserve requirement can be calculated once an organization has determined the five-year projected cash operating expenses for the plan period. This figure is obtained by dividing the fifth year cash operating expenses by 365 days to obtain a per day cash requirement. Multiply this per day requirement by the target days cash on hand of a similarly rated organization (obtained from agency data such as Table 2-1). This yields the organization's target cash reserve requirement.

How do we determine capital sources on the right side of the financial planning equation?

Capital sources include unrestricted cash, net available debt capacity, and any other sources such as bond-related construction funds. The current year figure for unrestricted cash should be the first capital source listed on the right side of the financial planning equation.

The second figure, net available debt capacity, can be calculated as follows: First, determine the cash flow available for debt service in the current year. Next, obtain from agency rating data the ratio for target debt service coverage of similarly rated organizations. Divide the cash flow available for debt service by the ratio to determine a maximum annual debt service allowable figure. Compare this figure to existing maximum annual debt service. The difference between the two will be net available debt capacity.

For example, an organization has an actual cash flow available for debt service of $50,400M in the current plan year. The target for debt service coverage ratio for similarly "A" ranked organizations is 3.9x. This yields a maximum annual debt service allowable of $50,400M divided by 3.9x, or $12,923M. The organization's existing maximum annual debt service is $13,500M; therefore, the organization effectively has $0 available for debt capacity.

What happens when we put it all together?

A *capital position analysis* (Figure 2-3) integrates the left and right sides of the financial planning equation. This analysis compares the uses and sources of funds and calculates the expected capital shortfall or, in very unusual circumstance, a capital surplus. Total capital requirements or *uses* for our example organization are $386,602M. Total capital *sources* are $177,697M. The estimated five-year capital shortfall is $208,905M. In other words, if the organization intends to spend capital of $150,000M and establish a minimum cash position of $216,202M, it must first develop a plan to close the cash shortfall of $208,905M during the next five years.

How do we determine the level of profitability necessary to close the cash shortfall?

The challenge at this point is to determine the level of cash flow needed to balance the financial equation. Figure 2-4 illustrates an organization's operating cash flow requirements for the five-year plan period at differing levels of capital investment. If this organization wants to invest $150,000M during the plan period, it must generate an average annual cash flow of $41,781M to close the cash shortfall.

This organization now must ask and answer a key question: "Is that level of cash flow attainable?" In other words, does the projected financial performance of the system under business-as-usual operating assumptions in fact support $150,000M capital investment over five years? If the answer to this question is "yes," then the strategies on which the plan is based are financially feasible given the organization's capabilities. The organization can confidently proceed with its intended strategy.

FIGURE 2-4.   2000–2004 Cash Flow Requirements (in Thousands)

Capital Investment Level FY 2000–2004	Required Cash Flow	
	Total Five Year	Average Annual
$100,000	$158,905	$31,781
$125,000	$183,905	$36,781
$150,000 (baseline)	$208,905	$41,781
$175,000	$233,905	$46,781
$200,000	$258,905	$51,781

FY 1999 Projected Cash Flow	*$34,001*
FY 1998 Projected Cash Flow	*$40,878*
FY 1997 Projected Cash Flow	*$50,701*

Source: Kaufman, Hall & Associates. Used with permission.

Figure 2-4 indicates that the answer to the question appears to be "no." The organization's cash flow has declined markedly in recent years from $50,701M in 1997 to 1999 projected cash flow of $34,001M. The required level of profitability is beyond the level of profitability achieved by the organization to date. Hence, the organization must ask another key question: "Could we make changes in our operations and strategies to achieve that level of profitability?" To close the capital shortfall and meet profitability targets, this organization will need to reduce capital spending, improve market share and revenues, or reduce operating costs. Without such changes, the organization's strategic plan would not be viable. New strategies with new financial projections would be required.

How do we test the reasonableness of the projections?

To ensure realistic projections, goals must be measurable and objective. Realistic profitability goals reflect the level of cash flow needed to meet all of the organization's financial requirements outlined in its strategic plan. The key question is, "Is it reasonable to expect this organization to operate at the projected level of profitability?" Financial forecasts and target and sensitivity analyses are helpful tools for testing the assumptions behind the financial plan for the organization's financial performance. These tools involve using best practices forecasting techniques by identifying risk points and developing "what if" scenarios for key operating indicators. For example, sensitivity analysis would explore the financial implications of "what if hospital inpatient volume or hospital productivity decreased? or, what if salary inflation rates were higher than projected?"

Using competitive benchmarks to test the realism of profitability goals is not recommended. Although one might find it tempting to focus on the operating margin experienced by similarly rated hospitals, this number would not be an appropriate profitability goal for an organization requiring considerable capital for a new facility, for example. This organization would require a much higher goal. If the organization aims for the 3.1 percent operating margin achieved by "Aa"-rated organizations, for example, it will fall far short of meeting its capital needs. Financial goals should be developed from the results of the financial plan. Benchmarking in this case puts the cart before the horse, requiring the development of a financial plan based on established goals.

How can my organization enhance the effective implementation of the financial plan?

Implementation of the financial plan can be enhanced by welcoming organization-wide input into the plan's development and providing the opportunity and enough information for every member of the organization to participate in achieving the plan's goals and objectives. Key constituencies — including management, the board, clinical staff, middle managers, the

> **SIDEBAR 2-5.   Additional Tips to Ensure the Effective Implementation of the Financial Plan**
>
> - Obtain board approval of the financial plan.
> - Integrate the financial plan and the annual budget.
> - Update the financial plan on an annual basis.
> - Ensure that the organization's accounting system can provide expense, revenue, and capital investment data for each program or unit.

community, and lenders—must understand the goals. Carefully prepared materials presenting organizational objectives and how the leadership plans to achieve them should be made available to key constituencies. Understanding provides an organization-wide sense of ownership in financial direction.

Additional safeguards to ensure the effective implementation of the financial plan appear in Sidebar 2-5.

A well-developed and executed financial plan is key to an organization's survival and success in the current healthcare environment. In the *Wizard of Oz,* Dorothy wakes up "in full color" and exclaims, "Gee, Toto, I don't think we're in Kansas anymore." It is indeed a different healthcare world.

References

Berger, S. 1999. *Fundamentals of Healthcare Financial Management,* 56. New York: McGraw-Hill.

Bruton, G. D., B. M. Oviatt, and L. K. Kallas-Bruton. 1995. "Strategic Planning in Hospitals: A Review and Proposal." *Health Care Management Review* 20 (3): 16–25.

Cleverley, W. O. 1992. *Essentials of Health Care Finance.* Gaithersburg, MD: Aspen Publishers.

Nowicki, M. 1999. *The Financial Management of Hospitals and Healthcare Organizations,* 157. Chicago: Health Administration Press.

Ernst & Young. 1996. *Navigating Through the Changing Currents.* Washington, D.C.: Ernst & Young.

Griffith, J. R. 1999. *The Well-Managed Healthcare Organization,* 546. Chicago: Health Administration Press.

Larson, L. 1999. "What Every Board Should Know." *Trustee* 52 (4): 4–8.

CONCEPT THREE

WHAT'S MY LINE? ANALYZING AND BOOSTING CREDITWORTHINESS

UTTER THE WORDS "credit rating," and most people shudder. Images spring to mind of credit card statements outlining obscene interest rates for unpaid bills, or, worse yet, of an embarrassing moment when credit was denied while trying to buy the latest software at the local computer store. Indeed, as an indication of America's preoccupation with credit ratings, America Online lets customers access their rating from the AOL home page to learn what the agencies are reporting about the status of their personal credit. Our sense of worth seems to be tied to our line of credit.

Why is creditworthiness important to my healthcare organization?

Is this angst different for a healthcare organization? Not really. An organization's long-term competitive position today is substantially dependent on its ability to raise affordable capital in the debt markets. An organization's board and management must attain and maintain a minimum credit rating that permits the organization to effectively compete in its marketplace. Simply stated, credit ratings matter. Why?

First, creditworthy organizations have improved capital market opportunities. One such opportunity is *access to credit enhancement* such as bond insurance or a letter/line of credit. By purchasing bond insurance or a line of credit, an organization in the "A" rated category or better essentially can "buy up" to a higher credit rating. A higher rating means lower interest costs.

29

A small decrease in the interest rate multiplied out over the life of the bond can mean significant savings. A single notch drop in a bond rating by Moody's, Fitch IBCA, or Standard & Poor's (see Sidebar 3-1) can mean a significant difference in the price of capital.

Second, creditworthy organizations also have *access to both taxable and tax-exempt debt.* Taxable debt may be required for certain programs or services that don't qualify for tax-exempt debt. Organizations with a strong credit rating ("A" or better) may want to exercise the option of taxable debt for investments such as physician office buildings or physician services and programs. Creditworthy organizations also can *access derivative options* such as interest rate swaps, caps, and other means or mechanisms to reduce overall interest rate costs and risk exposure.

Third, creditworthy organizations enjoy less *restrictive bond document covenants* which gives them the full benefit of financial flexibility. Lower-rated organizations are held to different standards that limit their flexibility to protect investors.

Fourth, creditworthy organizations also experience *lower costs associated with issuing their bonds.* Many of the large investor groups, funds, and insurance corporations that normally buy tax-exempt hospital bonds are precluded from buying debt beneath the "A"-rated category. Hence, the pool of potential investors for "BBB" bonds, for example, is much smaller than for higher-rated bonds. Selling to a larger pool simply takes less time and energy and results in lower issuance costs. Because of lower risk associated with issuing bonds for a creditworthy organization, insurance premiums are lower, as are letters and lines of credit from banks and underwriting and remarketing charges. In addition, organizations with impeccable credit often can issue their debt without setting aside a *debt service reserve fund*. Organizations with deteriorating credit will often be required to establish such a fund by setting aside at least a year's worth of principal and interest payments in an escrow account that cannot be accessed. This increases the amount of the borrowing, thereby increasing total principal and interest payments over the life of the bond.

Fifth and finally, *creditworthy organizations are market consolidators*. Organizations with the highest credit ratings are the most attractive partners to those with lower ratings. Such organizations offer excess capital capacity and lower capital costs. In the current healthcare environment, strong organizations are consolidating markets by acquiring or merging with weaker competitors that are often no longer able to compete because of a lack of access to cost-effective capital.

A summary of why credit ratings matter appears as Figure 3-1.

What factors are influencing access to capital in the current healthcare environment?

Numerous pressures currently influencing the healthcare industry are affecting the credit ratings of healthcare providers and thus their access to capital. Many of these pressures are systemic, and include:

- Declining profitability because of greater-than-expected revenue losses associated with the BBA of 1997;
- Declining reimbursement rates resulting from government initiatives to reduce healthcare expenditures and managed care cost constraints;

FIGURE 3-1. Why Credit Ratings Matter

Creditworthy organizations have improved capital market opportunities:

- Access to credit enhancement;
- Access to taxable or tax-exempt debt;
- Access to derivative options; and
- Less restrictive bond document covenants.

Creditworthy organizations have a lower cost of capital:

- "AAA" insured versus "Baa" interest rate spread ranges from approximately 30 to 40 basis points;
- Lower issuance costs: insurance premium, letter/line of credit, underwriting/ remarketing; and
- Avoidance of debt service reserve fund.

Creditworthy organizations are market consolidators:

- Nationwide, organizations with the highest credit rating have been the most attractive partners, have excess capital capacity, and exhibit the lowest cost of capital.

Source: Kaufman, Hall & Associates. Used with permission.

- Increasing costs associated with providing uncompensated care to an increasing proportion of uninsured U.S. patients;
- Increased government focus on industry coding practices;
- Increased competition resulting from industry consolidation;
- Increased salary, wages, and benefits expenses resulting from tighter labor markets;
- Losses from physician integration strategies; and
- An increasingly volatile stock market.

Selected pressures are described in more detail in the following paragraphs.

The *financial effects of the BBA 1997* were much greater than originally expected, particularly for hospitals, home health, long-term care, and rehabilitation facilities. The Congressional Budget Office now expects the freeze on hospital Medicare inpatient payment rates for fiscal year 1998 and the reduction in Medicare's expenditure growth through 2002 to generate more than $200 billion in savings. Providers are lobbying intensively for relief, but lower reimbursement levels are likely to continue contributing to providers' deteriorating credit quality and access to capital.

The continued growth of managed care creates unrelenting financial pressure for hospitals and other healthcare providers. The predominant strategy exercised by hospitals in the early 1990s was to sign as many managed care contracts as quickly as possible. This resulted in higher market share but often unprofitable arrangements. By the late 1990s, the new strategy to improve financial performance involved focusing on becoming the lowest-cost provider and exiting unprofitable arrangements. Managed care's ever-lower payment schedules and ever-slower claims payment (not to mention outright claims denial) continue to shrink hospital profitability margins, resulting in lower credit ratings and reduced access to capital.

Mergers, acquisitions, and affiliations show signs of slowing down as past deals have not met expectations. Healthcare transactions plummeted 42 percent between 1998 and 1999 (Bellandi 1999). Although market share and mission may have been enhanced through mergers and other affiliations, in many cases, costs have not been reduced to the extent projected. Credit downgrades often are driven by financial problems—such as shortcomings in receivables collections—resulting from the problematic integration of noncompatible management information systems. Allegheny Health and Education Research Foundation (AHERF) is often cited as an example of a provider that could not integrate its operations into a cohesive organization. Integration strategies are now becoming dis-integration strategies as providers rethink their organizational structures to ensure the financial health of core businesses. Nonperforming assets such as physician clinics and PHOs with employed physicians are being restructured or terminated. Acute care hospitals are eliminating losses associated with their purchase of nonacute care facilities such as home health agencies and long-term care facilities by divesting these entities.

What are the key determinants of creditworthiness? What do credit agencies review to determine an organization's credit rating?

During the past decade, rating agencies have shifted their focus from a microanalysis of organizations as stand-alone entities to a broader macroanalysis of organizations as part of complex regional and national healthcare systems. The agencies look at what they call "strategy" as critical to current rating assessments of not-for-profit healthcare entities. Strategy encompasses key creditworthiness factors broadly categorized as market position, financial performance, debt position, governance and management, and legal structure. Each is described below.

Market position involves gauging the degree to which the organization controls the marketplace. Is there significant competition? As competition increases, so does the risk to the organization's financial position. Is the organization able to compete for clinical services, physicians, covered lives, and care settings in a market with expanded geographic coverage? How attractive is the organization to managed care payers and how able is it to provide a full spectrum of services in the lowest possible cost setting (i.e., generally in outpatient sites)? Is the organization able to compete as a cost-effective provider? How effectively does the organization compete for physician loyalty to obtain patient referrals? What are the strategies and methods used by the healthcare organization to link the medical staff and their patients to the hospital and to increase the organization's primary care base? Is the local economy growing?

Financial performance and particularly *debt position* indicate an organization's ability to repay debt. The higher the debt, the lower the credit rating. Critical mass and consistency are important in the current healthcare environment. Credit agencies analyze systemwide rather than entity-specific operations through review of consolidated financial information. The focus is on cash flow generated from core operations and on the key ratios that incorporate cash flow. These factors go to the heart of the assessment of credit risk. The debt-to-cash flow ratio is of particular importance because

> ... it measures the relationship between the debt obligation and the
> ability to generate ongoing cash flow to service the debt. It also

provides an effective measure of leverage in that it captures the time period during which the hospital will have to maintain its current operating performance in order to pay back all of its debt by relating the balance sheet liability to recurring annual cash flow. All else being equal, the longer the time period that a hospital must service an obligation, the higher the ratio, and the riskier we perceive the timely repayment of the debt to be (Moody's Investor's Service 1999).

Key ratios measuring financial performance are described on pages 40–41.

On the revenue side, agencies review an organization's strategies for competing for managed care contracts and capitated arrangements and strategies to counter greater-than-expected revenue reductions. How cash balances are invested is important, as are the organization's dependence on non-operating income to bolster profit margins and ability to duplicate or exceed the current year's financial performance.

An organization's *governance and management* functions are highly scrutinized to establish and ensure accurate credit ratings. Effective leadership is critical to creditworthiness. Good managers and board members can make things happen; ineffective managers and board members cannot. Finding the right people is particularly critical for providers during periods of rapid change. Agencies are interested in determining whether management has developed or hired individuals with new skills and understanding to cope with new marketplace challenges and whether it has modified its operations to meet the challenges. Board members often are assessed to determine their ability to balance opportunities with sensible financial performance.

Finally, the organization's *legal structure* is key to protecting bondholders. If bondholders cannot gain direct access to the assets of an operating entity because of legal structure, credit risk increases. Agencies now consider the more traditional joint and several/obligated group structure for multientity healthcare issuers as a credit strength and the restricted-affiliate structure as a credit weakness. The latter transfers the legal obligation for public bonds from the primary operating entities to a parent holding company.

Sample financial factors tracked by each rating agency appear as Tables 3-1, 3-2, and 3-3.

**TABLE 3-1.   Freestanding Hospital and Single-State Healthcare Systems
Healthcare Medians by Rating Category, 1998***

	All Ratings	Aa	A	Baa	Below Baa
Distribution of Healthcare Ratings[†]	100%	11%	45%	36%	8%
Median Sample Size	303	35	142	114	12
Utilization					
Maintained beds	256	662	310	171	183
Admissions	12,208	35,559	15,124	7,940	7,062
Patient days	60,533	178,808	73,825	39,566	39,720
Average length of stay	5.0	5.2	4.9	4.9	5.2
Maintained bed occupancy	61.8%	69.6%	63.3%	58.1%	57.7%
Emergency room visits	37,566	73,393	43,853	26,101	30,946
Outpatient visits	118,629	236,091	135,168	94,069	46,388
Outpatient surgeries	5,459	12,362	7,533	4,161	4,187
Medicare case mix index	1.38	1.68	1.41	1.31	1.22
Financial Performance (in thousands)					
Net patient revenues	$121,932	$431,526	$147,151	$77,019	$63,657
Total operating revenue	132,601	470,244	154,303	82,987	65,540
Interest expense	2,897	9,372	3,222	2,138	2,425
Depreciation and amortization expense	8,278	29,613	9,815	4,726	3,755
Total operating expenses	131,285	440,574	151,776	81,029	69,961
Income from operations	2,131	12,805	3,260	949	296
Excess of revenue over expenses	6,246	39,327	10,068	2,489	1,663
Net revenue available for debt service	17,871	79,059	23,869	9,788	7,779
Operating cash flow	12,631	58,269	17,996	7,570	7,598
Debt service	4,938	11,371	5,763	3,620	3,117
Additions to property, plant, and equipment	12,621	48,359	16,257	5,933	2,258
Balance Sheet (in thousands)					
Unrestricted cash and investments	$53,683	$328,087	$79,776	$23,937	$11,984
Restricted cash and investments	3,271	19,284	5,083	1,697	211
Net fixed assets	78,165	287,849	97,031	45,555	36,324
Long-term debt	60,010	232,294	68,203	34,081	31,919
Debt service reserve and debt service funds	4,489	5,967	5,231	3,696	3,258
Net debt	50,000	157,455	58,968	29,039	28,704
Unrestricted fund balance	90,363	477,057	132,868	46,778	24,951

TABLE 3-1. (continued)

	All Ratings	Aa	A	Baa	Below Baa
Key Ratios					
Operating margin	2.2%	3.1%	2.6%	1.3%	0.5%
Excess margin	4.9%	7.7%	6.2%	3.3%	1.9%
Operating cash flow margin	10.3%	11.0%	10.8%	9.7%	8.4%
Return on assets	4.2%	5.3%	4.8%	2.9%	1.7%
Annual debt service coverage (x)	3.67	7.23	4.40	2.82	2.02
Maximum annual debt service coverage (x)	3.53	5.38	4.07	2.90	1.84
Current ratio (x)	2.0	1.8	2.1	2.0	1.5
Cash on hand (days)	154.6	255.2	200.5	100.2	39.9
Cushion ratio (x)	11.2	20.6	12.8	6.9	1.8
Cash-to-debt	98.7%	183.6%	115.4%	64.8%	22.4%
Accounts receivable (days)	64.2	66.6	64.0	64.2	59.2
Average payment period (days)	65.1	70.0	63.2	63.9	70.4
Debt-to-capitalization	37.7%	28.7%	35.4%	45.5%	63.1%
Debt-to-cash flow (x)	3.60	2.64	3.29	4.55	6.18
Average age of plant (years)	8.7	8.0	8.5	9.6	9.8
Patient Revenue Sources by Gross Revenue (%)[‡]					
Medicare	42.9	37.2	43.0	43.3	50.3
Medicaid	8.8	10.2	9.0	8.0	7.7
Blue Cross	8.5	8.2	10.0	8.1	6.6
Commercial	9.6	14.4	9.0	9.2	4.5
Managed Care	22.1	24.2	24.8	20.6	18.2
Self-pay and other	8.0	11.0	8.3	7.3	9.7

*Statistics are based on a sample size of 303 hospitals, excluding multistate hospital systems.

†Distribution encompasses all noninsured ratings as of 8/16/99, rather than the median sample.

‡Columns do not necessarily sum to 100 percent because each entry is a separately calculated median.

Source: Moody's Investors Service. 1999. *Not-for-Profit Health Care: 1999 Outlook and Medians.* New York: Moody's Investors Service. Used with permission.

TABLE 3-2. Not-for-Profit Healthcare Medians by Category

	AA+ to AA-		A+ to A-		BBB+ to BBB-	
	1999	*1998*	*1999*	*1998*	*1999*	*1998*
Utilization						
Average daily census	660	439	160	157	81	78
Statement of Operations						
Net patient revenue (thousands)	543,564	382,415	136,509	118,487	59,810	53,490
Salaries & benefits/net patient rev (%)	53.6	51.4	51.0	50.3	51.7	50.7
Bad debts exp/total oper rev (%)	3.5	3.4	4.3	4.3	4.9	4.6
Max debt serv cov (x)	4.3	5.2	3.7	4.1	3.0	3.3
Max debt sevice to total oper rev (%)	3.0	3.4	3.5	3.8	4.4	4.3
Interest coverage (x)	8.2	8.4	6.8	6.9	4.5	5.3
EBIDA ($000s)	96,368	75,617	24,532	21,317	7,379	8,623
Non oper rev/total rev (%)	4.4	4.3	3.5	3.2	2.0	2.0
EBIDA margin (%)	14.5	16.1	13.7	14.7	12.1	13.6
Operating margin (%)	2.9	3.8	2.2	4.6	1.5	3.3
Profit margin (%)	6.5	7.9	5.5	7.3	3.6	5.2
Balance Sheet						
Avg age net fixed assets (years)	8.6	8.1	8.7	8.5	9.2	8.8
Cushion ratio (x)	17.6	17.1	11.4	10.8	6.8	5.9
Days cash on hand	212	211	167	168	112	117
Days in accounts receivable	67.2	63.1	64.6	61.2	64.1	60.8
Cash flow/total liabilities (%)	21.6	24.5	20.6	22.3	15.8	19
Unrestricted cash/long term debt (%)	146	153	108	116	67	72
Long-term debt/capitalization (%)	30.1	31.7	33.9	34.3	42.6	40.5
Payment period (days)	66.5	69.8	65.3	63.6	64.1	61.4

1999 medians based on 1998 audited financials. 1998 medians based on 1997 audited financials.

Source: Standard & Poor's. 1999. *Standard & Poor's Credit Week Municipal.* October 25. Reprinted with permission.

TABLE 3-3.   1999 Medians

Medians	All	Aa	A	Bbb	Below Bbb
Net patient revenues ($mil.)	146.0	640.0	96.5	65.0	94.0
Days cash on hand	151.5	221.0	169.9	97.3	54.1
Days in accounts receivables	64.6	68.2	64.9	62.7	52.1
Cushion ratio (x)	9.7	16.6	10.6	5.4	2.7
Days in current liabilities	67.7	68.0	65.0	68.8	68.2
Cash to debt (%)	93.6	155.3	100.2	58.8	28.1
Operating margin (%)	2.7	3.7	3.4	1.6	(1.2)
Excess margin (%)	5.0	7.7	5.6	2.5	0.7
EBITDA margin (%)	12.5	15.4	13.8	10.5	12.5
CFFOBI margin (%)	11.3	12.5	11.5	9.2	11.2
EBITDA debt service coverage (x)	3.4	4.5	3.5	2.6	1.6
CFFOBI debt service coverage (x)	2.9	3.7	3.0	2.4	1.8
CFFOBI coverage less capital expenditures (x)	0.9	1.4	0.4	0.7	1.1
MADS as percent of revenues	3.9	3.5	4.2	3.9	6.5
Debt to EBITDA (x)	3.0	2.5	2.8	3.8	6.3
Debt to capitalization (%)	36.7	32.7	35.8	43.5	69.7
Debt to NPP&E	79.5	74.0	78.2	81.8	101.2
Debt to assets (%)	29.8	25.4	30.9	31.1	55.0
Average age of plant (years)	8.9	8.9	8.7	9.5	9.3

EBITDA: earnings before interest, taxes, depreciation, and amortization

MADS: maximum annual debt service

NPP&E: net property, plant, and equipment

CFFOBI: cash flow from operations before interest

Source: Fitch IBCA, Inc. 1999. "1999 Financial Median." Special Report. Reprinted by permission of Fitch IBCA, Inc.

What financial factors affect creditworthiness?

The creditworthiness of a healthcare organization is determined by its financial performance. Dozens of factors are relevant to financial performance; the challenge is to select those most indicative of the organization's financial strengths and weaknesses. The following eight indicators provide an effective measure:

1. Operating margin, which reflects the profitability from operations;
2. Excess margin, which reflects profitability from operations and non-operating revenue;
3. Debt service coverage, which measures how cash flow covers debt service;
4. Debt-to-capitalization ratio, which indicates how highly leveraged, or debt financed, the organization is: the higher the capitalization ratio, the higher the risk;
5. Cushion ratio compares the organization's free cash to its annual debt service;
6. Days cash on hand, another gauge of liquidity and probably the most important credit ratio in use today, reflects the number of days of cash set aside by the organization to cover operating expenses;
7. Average days in accounts receivable measures the timeliness of collections and is widely considered to be an accurate barometer of financial management; and
8. Average age of plant measures the age of physical facilities and technology and provides perspective on the organization's need for capital.

Each indicator can be expressed as a ratio (see next question).

Which ratios should be used to analyze creditworthiness?

The financial ratios reflecting each indicator mentioned above are as follows:

1. Operating margin:

$$\frac{\text{Total operating revenue} - \text{Operating expenses}}{\text{Total operating revenue}}$$

2. Excess margin:

$$\frac{\text{Income from operations} + \text{Non-operating revenue}}{\text{Total operating} + \text{Non-operating revenue}}$$

3. Debt service coverage:

$$\frac{\text{Excess revenue over expenses} + \text{Depreciation} + \text{Interest} + \text{Amortization}}{\text{Annual debt service}}$$

4. Capitalization ratio:

$$\frac{\text{Long-term debt (less current portion)}}{\text{Long-term debt (less current portion)} + \text{Net assets}}$$

5. Average days in accounts receivable (net):

$$\frac{(\text{Accounts receivable net of reserves})}{(\text{Net patient revenue less bad debt expense})} \times 365$$

6. Cushion ratio:

$$\frac{\text{Cash and marketable securities} + \text{Board designated funds}}{\text{Annual debt service}}$$

7. Days cash on hand:

$$\frac{\text{Cash and marketable securities} + \text{Board designated funds}}{\text{Total operating expenses} - \text{Depreciation}} \times 365$$

8. Average age of plant:

$$\frac{\text{Accumulated depreciation}}{\text{Depreciation expense}}$$

FIGURE 3-2. Creditworthiness Comments

- Very strong, relatively stable liquidity position (380 days cash on hand).
- Cash reserves are the system's primary source of credit strength and profitability (interest earnings).
- Overall decline in profitability and operating cash flow (EBITDA)
  - Managed care discounting pressures and Medicare reductions have driven collection rates from 66.9 percent to 57.9 percent over three years.
  - Compensation ratio has risen from 53.3 percent to 57.7 percent over three years.
  - 1998 results include one-time costs associated with information system conversion and project opening.
- Debt-related ratios are very strong (6.9 multiplied by debt service coverage and 20.6 percent debt-to-capitalization)
  - All-in cost debt capital has been extremely low at 4 percent.
- Facility condition is excellent as evidenced by low average age of plant of 7.5 years.
- Maintaining "AA" profile will be difficult without improving operating performance.

How do we perform a financial credit analysis?

A financial credit analysis allows your organization to compare its recent financial performance to relevant national standards that serve as a benchmark. Organizations typically use key indicators from Standard & Poor's, Fitch IBCA's, or Moody's for similarly rated organizations to construct the necessary data chart. These indicators include revenue, income, cash, and debt figures as well as profitability, debt, and liquidity ratios.

Table 3-4 provides a financial credit analysis chart for an "AA"-rated organization. An analysis of the data enables your organization to draw conclusions or make key observations about relative performance. Observations about this organization appear as Figure 3-2.

What do credit agencies foresee for healthcare organizations in the future? Sidebar 3-2 provides rating agency forecasts at the turn of the century.

TABLE 3-4. Financial Credit Analysis Highlights (in Thousands of Dollars)

Ratio/Statistic	Moody's "AA" Rated Hospital*	S&P's "AA" Rated Hospital[†]	Community Hospital[‡]			
			Actual 1997	Actual 1998	Actual 1999	Projected 2000
Net patient revenue	$394,186	$382,415	$191,495	$195,303	$196,724	$202,358
Operating income[§]	—	—	$11,356	$7,167	$(1,017)	$(807)
Net income	$40,126	—	$39,840	$31,421	$16,475	$16,264
Net income + depreciation	$70,446	—	$52,513	$45,465	$33,583	$36,440
EBITDA"	$79,706	$75,617	$55,420	$49,364	$37,402	$40,266
Unrestricted cash	$270,238	—	$184,874	$200,774	$202,976	$204,506
Long-term debt	$184,977	—	$84,512	$94,711	$92,804	$90,811
Operating income[§]	3.4%	3.8%	5.7%	3.5%	(0.5)%	(0.4)%
Excess margin	7.9%	7.9%	17.5%	13.7%	7.3%	7.0%
EBITDA margin	—	16.1%	24.4%	21.5%	16.5%	17.3%
Debt service coverage	5.4x	5.2x	12.3x	9.0x	6.7x	6.9x
Debt to capitalization	28.2%	31.7%	22.7%	23.1%	21.8%	20.6%
Cushion ratio	17.3x	17.1x	41.0x	36.5x	36.1x	35.3x
Days cash on hand	200.8	210.9	386	398	384	380
Days in accounts receivable	61.4	63.1	70	71	103	85
Average age of plant (years)	7.5	8.1	7.9	8.2	7.8	7.5
Compensation ratio	—	51.4%	53.3%	53.2%	54.9%	57.7%
Net patient revenue/ gross charges	—	—	66.9%	65.0%	61.7%	57.9%

*Reflects Moody's medians for hospitals rated in the "Aa" category in 1997.
†Reflects Standard & Poor's medians for hospitals rated in the "AA" category in 1997.
‡Excludes the Foundation and Health Services.
§Includes approximately $3 million of investment income on operations reserve fund.
"EBITDA: earnings before interest, taxes, depreciation, and amoritization.

SIDEBAR 3-2.   The Future Credit Outlook for Healthcare Organizations
According to the Rating Agencies

Whenever experts try to predict the future, forecasts vary and are short-lived. What is predicted this month may be absolutely wrong by next month. In a rapidly changing environment, even short-term forecasts are likely to be inaccurate; medium-term outlooks are akin to predictions gained through gazing into crystal balls. The following forecasts were provided by three major credit agencies. They are to be taken with a liberal grain of salt, because by this book's publication, they will be proof of the fleeting nature of predictions.

Fitch IBCA (Kaufman Hall 1999) expects continued decline in operating performance of healthcare organizations and a decline in excess income because of market forces. The agency expects liquidity improvements to fall off because of weakened financial performance, continued capital expenditures, and other factors. The agency expects consolidations and affiliations to continue, but at a slower pace because the most sensible ones have already occurred. Significant savings from mergers are not forecasted. The agency believes that healthcare systems with clout will exit unprofitable managed care contracts, and those without clout will exit only if their management information systems enable them to track profitability by contract. Judicious hospitals are expected to seek market share only if it results in improved profitability. Hospitals will divest themselves of nonacute care entities with the exception of employed physicians.

Moody's Investor's Service (1999) expects that the not-for-profit healthcare sector's high ratings volatility and deteriorating credit quality will continue into the millennium. The agency's prognosis is for further credit deterioration, even for some highly rated providers. The overall outlook for the nearly 500 not-for-profit hospitals and systems rated by the agency is negative. Over the longer term, Moody's predicts greater credit stability overall for providers as they become larger, more efficient, better integrated, and focused on core operations. The agency's rating distribution for the organizations it rates appears as Model 3-1. The average median rating for the sector currently stands at "A3." If the current trends continue, Moody's

(continued on following page)

SIDEBAR 3-2. (continued)

MODEL 3-1.   Rating Distribution

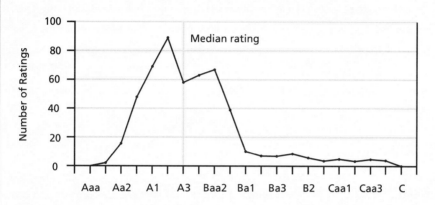

As of August 6, 1999

Source: Moody's Investors Service 1999. *Rating Methodology: Moody's Evolving Credit Analysis of U.S. Not-for-Profit Hospitals,* June, 5.

indicates that the median rating could decline to "Baa1" within the inter-mediate term (three to four years).

Standard and Poor's (S&P 1999) expects continued pressure on ratings for at least the near and medium term, but offers some hope for the future. Optimism for the industry comes from decreased capitated revenues and related risk, the divestiture of noncore services, and the increased financial flexibility of healthcare organizations at each rating level. Three S&P exec-utives describe:

> Financial ratios are stronger in all ways versus the ratios ten years ago. For example, the "A" median in 1989 for days' cash was 66, compared with 162 currently. In many ways, hospitals now have a better shot—at least financially—at addressing the issues than ever before. In addition, hospitals have demonstrated an irrepressible ability to adapt to the industry's constantly changing environment, and there have been very few defaults historically.

What is the take-home message about creditworthiness?

Credit and creditworthiness are enduring concepts. Healthcare organizations that understand the importance of creditworthiness and maintain a strong credit position will do well in the future. Those that neither understand the factors underlying creditworthiness nor maintain a strong credit position are operating in uncertain and perilous circumstances. Their future is bleak. In today's healthcare organization, finance had better be the line of work practiced by the "mystery man" in the popular *What's My Line* television show of past decades.

References

Bellandi, D. 1999. "Let's Not Make a Deal." *Modern Healthcare* 29 (43): 20.

Kaufman Hall. 1999. Adapted from presentation by Jordan Melick during Kaufman Hall 10th Annual Financial Leadership Conference: "Learning from the Leaders." 20–22 October.

Moody's Investors Service. 1999. *Rating Methodology: Moody's Evolving Credit Analysis of U.S. Not-for-Profit Hospitals* [Pamphlet]. June.

Standard & Poor's. 1999. *Credit Week Municipal* [Pamphlet]. October 25.

CONCEPT FOUR

Hazards ahead: estimating, taking, and managing risk

Sam L. Savage, PH.D.

Director, Industrial Affiliates Program and Senior Research Associate,
Department of Management Science and Engineering,
Stanford University, Stanford, California

"THE ONLY CERTAINTY," a Roman scholar once said, is that "nothing is certain." Of course most professionals have had a course in statistics at some point in their lives to help them deal with uncertainty. Unfortunately, what most people learn from their statistics course is that they do not like and do not understand statistics. The good news is that new computerized techniques are revolutionizing the way we visualize uncertainty and manage risk. These new techniques, pioneered on Wall Street for managing financial assets, are now beginning to be applied to a broad range of industries, including healthcare.

What is the difference between risk and uncertainty?

People often use the terms "risk" and "uncertainty" interchangeably and imprecisely. Uncertainty is an objective feature of the universe, while risk is in the eye of the beholder. For example, consider an uncertainty involving future government funding of healthcare program X. The objective uncertainty is that funding for X will either go up or down. Everyone is in the

---

Readers are advised to take a bit more time with this chapter. It provides concise information on analytical techniques that will be critical to future financial decision making in a difficult healthcare environment.

same state of uncertainty. But the risk associated with this uncertainty depends on who you are. Consider the financial risk from the perspective of three stakeholders as shown in the table below.

Stakeholder	*Risk Associated with the Uncertainty*
A hospital with a continuing program in X.	Potential cash shortfall if government reduces funding for X.
A hospital with a continuing program in Y, which competes for funding with X.	Potential cash shortfall if government increases funding for X.
A hospital with neither a program in X or Y.	None

The first stage of risk management is to gain a better understanding of the uncertainties with which your risks are associated. It is tempting to gloss over uncertainties, for example, by simply planning for the "average" case. The right way to manage risk, however, is to face up to uncertainty and explicitly acknowledge and plan for various possible outcomes.

What are some important sources of risk?

There are, of course, many types of uncertainties with which risks are associated. The list below is far from exhaustive. It is meant to serve as a starting point for your own list.

- *Uncertain government action.* The funding example above is in this category.
- *Competition.* Will your organization still be viable if a new healthcare provider comes to town?
- *Local economic factors.* What will happen to your bottom line if a major local employer moves its headquarters to another part of the country?

- *Global economic factors.* How would your finances be affected by a recession?
- *Interest rate.* If interest rates go up, will you still be able to service your debt?
- *Wage rate inflation.* If healthcare wages increase more rapidly than the general price index, how will you meet your payroll?
- *Capacity constraints.* Suppose demand for your services is overwhelming. Will you be able to fill it?
- *Capitation risk.* If the need for a specific expensive procedure exceeds the estimate for your capitated population, how will you cover the shortfall?

Remember this list is a starting point only. Your own list is the one that counts the most.

How can uncertainty and risk be visualized?

What will your bottom line be next year, or five years from now? You do not know exactly of course, but if you are like most people you will try to come up with a number that serves as a best guess. A better approach is to explicitly estimate a range of outcomes instead of a single number. For example, suppose your best guess for next year's bottom line is $1 million, but when push comes to shove, you have to admit that it conceivably might range between a high of a $2,250,000 profit to a loss of $250,000. Your gut tells you that there is only one chance in twenty, that is 5 percent, that either extreme could occur, but neither is out of the question. Well, if this is what you feel, do not hide behind the single number of $1 million. Start thinking of the whole picture as shown in Figure 4-1.

Histograms

A histogram (as displayed in Figure 4-1) is a more realistic picture of your bottom line than the single number $1,000,000. Risk estimation is basically the art and science of coming up with more accurate pictures like that

FIGURE 4-1.   Histogram of Estimated Bottom Line

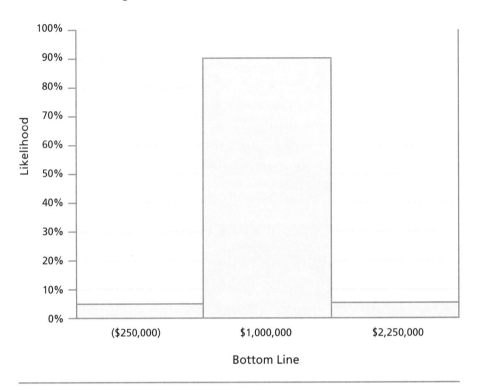

in Figure 4-1. The remainder of this section will describe some of the ways you can obtain a more accurate picture along with things you can do to manage risk once it has been estimated. For now, imagine that through more detailed study, you and your colleagues arrive at the more refined histogram shown in Figure 4-2.

Notice that in each histogram, the bars must total 100 percent. This is just another way of saying that of all the outcomes you have considered, one of them must occur.

Technically speaking, the *average* of a distribution is just the point at which the histogram would *balance* if it were made of a solid material. The *expected value* and *mean* are equivalent terms for the average. The *mode* is the location of the highest bar on the histogram, and the *median* is the point at

FIGURE 4-2. Refined Histogram of Estimated Bottom Line

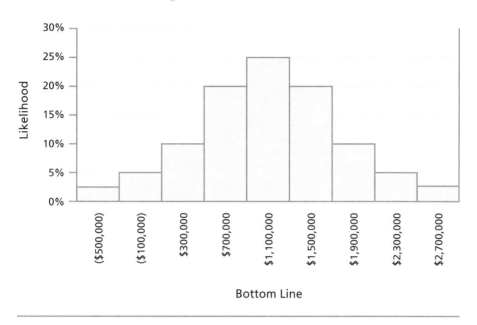

which exactly half the mass lies to the right or left. These terms are often confused, which is why it is so tempting to use them for purposes of obfuscation. For a full discussion of this topic, readers may wish to consult Darrell Huff's classic *How to Lie with Statistics* (1993).

Although histograms do tell the story of uncertainty, risk analysts often use a closely related graph called the cumulative graph. Instead of showing the likelihood of some specific range of outcomes occuring, the cumulative graph (Figure 4-3) displays the likelihood that the bottom line is a certain amount or *less*. For example, the likelihood of the bottom line being $300,000 or less is 17.5 percent, which is calculated by adding up the first three bars of the histogram in Figure 4-2. Histograms and cumulative graphs are different ways to view the distribution of an uncertain number.

The greater the number of bars in the graphs, the smoother the picture of the distribution. Figures 4-4a and 4-4b display the distributions for Figures 4-2 and 4-3 with an increased number of bars. In conclusion, how is

FIGURE 4-3. Cumulative Graph of Estimated Bottom Line

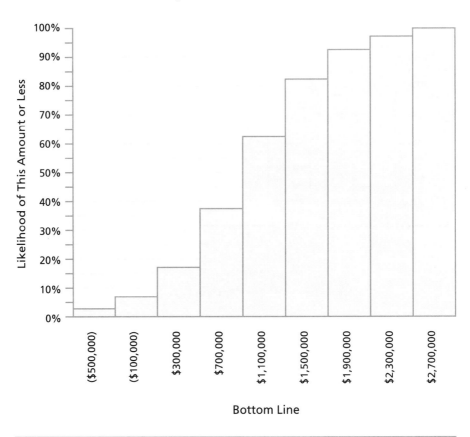

risk estimated? With distributions, not single numbers. And distributions can be viewed as shapes that provide a quick picture of the whole range of possible outcomes.

Value at risk

Traditionally risk has been measured in terms of variance, an unintuitive mathematical calculation that was about the best one could do in the pre-computer age. Value at risk is a newer and clearer measure of risk that

FIGURES 4-4a.   Histogram Distribution In Greater Detail

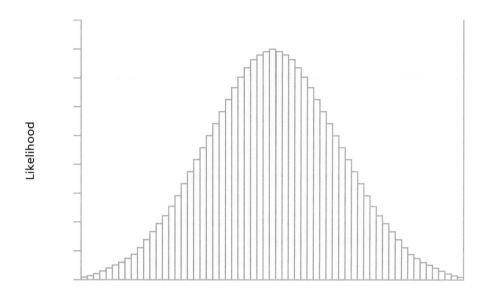

FIGURES 4-4b.   Cumulative Graph Distribution in Greater Detail

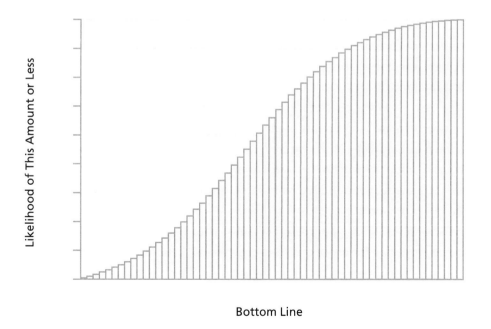

Bottom Line

represents a single point on the cumulative graph. For example, in Figure 4-3, the value at risk at 7.5 percent is $100,000. This means that there is a 7.5 percent chance of losing $100,000 or more. It is tempting, when comparing the risk of two investments, to just compare their value at risk at some particular level, say 10 percent. But this can be misleading, because the investment with the lowest value at risk at 10 percent might have a higher value at risk at 5 percent. It is better therefore to compare the value at risk of the projects at more than one percentile.

How does diversification reduce risks?

Suppose you are responsible for all surgeries of a certain type with a capitated group of 100 individuals. Suppose this surgery is required for 10 percent of the general population each year. The actual percentage requiring the surgery among your group in the upcoming year may be greater or less than 10 percent as reflected in Figure 4-5a. To avoid the risk of a cash shortfall, you have included a safety margin by budgeting for up to 15 percent of the patient population requiring the surgery. Your risk analyst calculates that you can now be 95 percent sure of not blowing your budget. That is, 95 percent of the total of the bars lie below 15 percent as in Figure 4-5a. If you were responsible for the same surgery over a capitated group of 1,000 instead of 100 individuals, you would again expect 10 percent to require the surgery. In this case, however, the actual amount would be expected to be much closer to the estimated 10 percent than it was with the smaller capitated group as shown in Figure 4-5b. If you budgeted for 15 percent of the population to require surgeries within the larger group, you would be 99.999 percent sure of not blowing your budget. That is, 99.999 percent of the total of the bars lie below 15 percent as shown in Figure 4-5b. Conversely, if you were still willing to live with 95 percent certainty, your budget could be reduced to cover surgeries for around 11.5% of the group. That is, 95% of the total of the bars lie below 11.5 percent in Figure 4-5b. The lesson here is that as you diversify over larger and larger sets of uncertainties, your percentage risk is reduced. This is the primary reason why bigger is better when it comes to the size of your capitated group.

FIGURES 4-5a. Distribution of Estimated Need for Surgery for a Population of 100

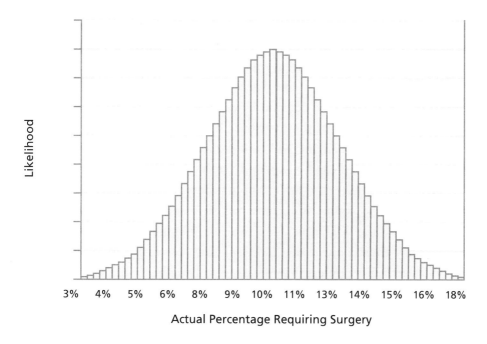

Actual Percentage Requiring Surgery

FIGURES 4-5b. Distribution of Estimated Need for Surgery for a Population of 1,000

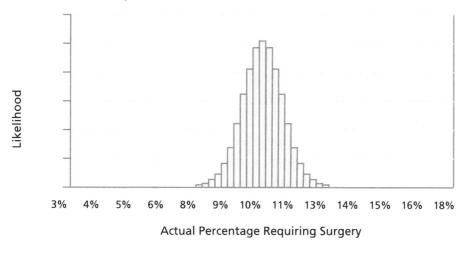

Actual Percentage Requiring Surgery

What is wrong with using averages in financial projections?

I use the term "flaw of averages" to describe the common planning errors that occur when "average" values of uncertainties are plugged into financial plans. Two simplified examples of one-year project plans are presented. The plans are for two different medical procedures, but each one yields revenue of $1,000 per patient. The demand for each procedure is uncertain, but the best guess, or average of the distribution, is 2000 patients in each case. Assume that actual demand will vary symmetrically around this average, but that the demand can be expected, with 95 percent confidence, to lie somewhere between 1,000 and 3,000 patients. For simplicity, we will assume that all uncertainty in demand will be resolved the day the clinic is opened for business. That is, if the expected number of patients show up the first day, then you will have 2,000 patients requiring the procedure in the full year. If more or less than the expected number of patients show up, then you will have more or less than 2,000 in the full year. Each plan requires an investment of $1,600,000 over the year. The projects, although they seem very similar on the surface, have important differences, as described below.

Project 1: Capital Intensive with Limited Capacity

1. Average demand has been plugged into the project plan as shown in Figure 4-6.
2. Capacity for the proposed clinic costs $800 per patient, so a $1,600,000 investment is planned to achieve the desired capacity of 2,000.
3. The total expected revenue is $1,000 multiplied by the expected number of patients, or $2,000,000, right?
4. Expected profit will therefore be $400,000, right?

Wrong and wrong! Here's why: Assume that 2,000 is indeed the best guess for demand, and that you have a fifty-fifty chance that it will be either higher or lower in actuality. In such a case, 50 percent of the time actual

FIGURE 4-6. Capital Intensive with Limited Capacity

	A	B	C	D	E
1	HEALTH CARE PROJECT PLAN				
2	Capital Intensive, with limited capacity				
3					
4	Estimated Demand (Patient Days)				
5			2000		
6					
7	Investment				
8	@ $800/Patient Day		$1,600,000		
9	Capacity		2000		
10					
11	Total Revenue				
12	@ $1,000/Patient Day		$2,000,000		
13					
14	Profit		$400,000		
15					
16					
17					
18					
19					
20					

Sheet1 / Sheet2 / Sheet3 /

demand will be less than 2,000 and profit will be less than $400,000. In fact, you could lose a lot of money if demand fell short of 1,600. But, of course, in the 50 percent chance that demand is greater than 2,000, profit will *not* be greater than $400,000 because the clinic only has a capacity of 2,000. Therefore, profit will be either exactly $400,000 or less than $400,000. Average profit cannot be $400,000, even though average demand is 2,000.

In this classic case of the flaw of averages, the average values of uncertainties plugged into financial models are wrongly assumed to yield average bottom lines. This one error is responsible for much bad planning throughout healthcare and other industries. Later we will discuss how simulation can provide more accurate results, but first, let us look at project 2.

FIGURE 4-7.   Operational Intensive with Option to Abandon

	A	B	C	D	E
1	HEALTH CARE PROJECT PLAN				
2	Operational Intensive, with option to abandon				
3					
4	Estimated Demand (Patient Days)				
5			2000		
6					
7	Investment				
8	Operating Expense		$1,600,000		
9					
10					
11	Total Revenue				
12	@ $1,000/Patient Day		$2,000,000		
13					
14	Profit		$400,000		
15					
16					
17					
18					
19					
20					

Sheet1 / Sheet2 / Sheet3 /

Project 2: Operation Intensive with Option to Abandon

1. Average demand has been plugged into the project plan as shown in Figure 4-7, just as with project 1.
2. All the costs are operational, with a total of $1,600,000 for the year and no limit to capacity.
3. The total expected revenue is $1,000 times the expected number of patients, or $2,000,000 — or is it?
4. Will the expected profit be $400,000?

Actually, the expected profit will be greater than $400,000! Can you explain why?

Suppose demand exceeds 2,000, then clearly profit will be greater than $400,000 (with this example, we do not have a capacity problem). If demand reached 3,000, for example, profit would be $1,400,000. Will this be balanced out by the likelihood that demand is less than 2,000? No. Any demand between 1,600 and 2,000 will be exactly balanced by demand between 2,000 and 2,400. However, if demand is less than $1,600, we would abandon the business rather than lose money. The upside represented by demand between 2,400 and 3,000 goes unbalanced on the downside and the expected profit is greater than $400,000. This is the notion behind real options. The option to abandon is worth a great deal in a case like this when it allows us to avoid potential losses.

In summary, when the average demand of 2,000 patients was plugged into either of these models, the resulting profit was $400,000. In the first case, the true average profit was considerably less than that amount, and in the second case it was considerably greater.

How can simulation be used to analyze uncertainty?

Monte Carlo simulation is a method of analyzing uncertainty that was developed during the Manhattan atomic bomb project. This method showers your model with thousands of random inputs while tracking the values of your outputs. The application of Monte Carlo simulation to business risk was popularized by David B. Hertz, in an article in the *Harvard Business Review* in 1964. Today, this technique can be accomplished in a spreadsheet model with only a few keystrokes. In the project examples described earlier, the inputs are the demands and the outputs are the profit cells. Both models were simulated with 5,000 random demands drawn from a bell-shaped distribution with an average of 2,000 patients and a 95-percent confidence interval of from 1,000 to 3,000 patients as shown in Figure 4-8. The resulting distributions of profit for the two projects are shown in Figures 4-9a and 4-9b.

Notice how the shapes of the distributions differ. Project 1 has the potential to lose a lot of money, and in the best case makes only $400,000. Project 2 has the potential to make a lot of money and in the worst case it will return zero. Note that once spreadsheet models of the plans had been created, the Monte Carlo simulation required only a few additional keystrokes.

FIGURE 4-8.   Simulated Demand (In Thousands)

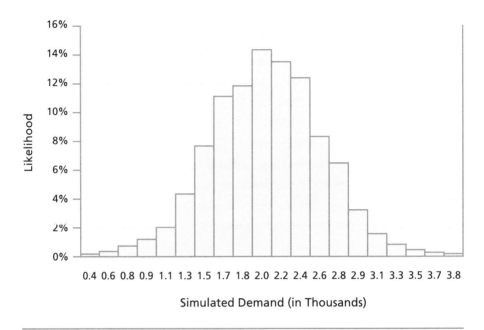

How can we best evaluate healthcare projects, given uncertainty?

A manager in charge of evaluating a healthcare project with uncertain demand has been asked to estimate profit. Depending on the response to this request I rank the manager's level of "stochastic enlightenment" as follows.

- If the manager answers: "I do not know what profit will be because I do not know what demand will be," I rank the manager at level 0, or "needs enlightenment."
- If the manager plugs in the average demand (in our examples, 2,000) and uses the resulting profit as his or her estimate, I rank the manager at level minus 1, or "in dire need of enlightenment." Note, in many organizations this is accepted practice.

FIGURE 4-9a.   Simulated Profit of Project 1

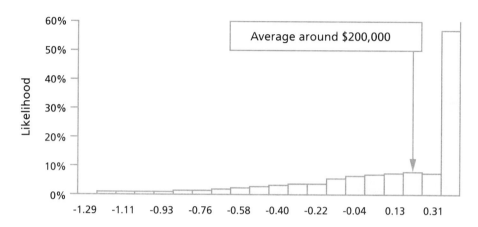

FIGURE 4-9b.   Simulated Profit of Project 2

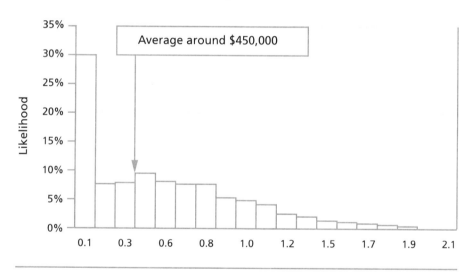

- If the manager explicitly takes into account the uncertainty, for example, by running a simulation, and gives a range of outcomes, I rank the manager at level 1, or "enlightened."

The description of how to reach a higher or proactive level of enlightenment (level 2) follows.

TABLE 4-1. Investment Versus Capacity in Project 1

Investment	Capacity
$800,000	1,000
$1,000,000	1,250
$1,200,000	1,500
$1,400,000	1,750
$1,600,000	2,000
$1,800,000	2,250

When taking risks, we should explicitly recognize the range of uncertainty of the inputs to our model and understand at least qualitatively how these uncertainties will affect the range of uncertainty in the outputs.

But we can go further than this by proactively experimenting with our plan in the face of uncertainty. For example, what would project 1 look like under different levels of investment? It is easy to run multiple simulations to find out.

Let us see what happens with six levels of investment and their associated levels of patient capacity as shown in Table 4-1.

The results of repeating the simulation for each of these investment levels are illustrated in Table 4-2 and graphically displayed in Figure 4-10. Note that the original investment of $1,600,000 seemed reasonable because it provided a capacity sufficient for the average demand and, seemingly, an average profit of $400,000. In reality, not only does that investment return an average profit of just $190,000, but it subjects the investors to a 5 percent chance of losing $420,000 or more! By investing $1,200,000, the average profit increases to $260,000 and the 5 percent value at risk simultaneously decreases to $20,000. Sure, go ahead and keep using averages in your business plans, but just don't come to me looking for an investment! For a further discussion of Monte Carlo simulation in spreadsheets see *insight.xla* (Savage 1998).

TABLE 4-2.   Average Profit and Value at Risk by Investment Level ($)

Investment level	Average profit	5 percent value at risk
$800,000	$190,000	190,000
$1,000,000	$230,000	180,000
$1,200,000	$260,000	(20,000)
$1,400,000	$240,000	(220,000)
$1,600,000	$190,000	(420,000)
$1,800,000	$90,000	(620,000)

FIGURE 4-10.   Value at Risk by Investment Level

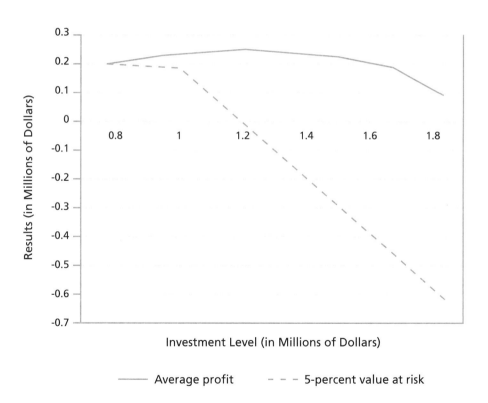

TABLE 4-3. Profiles of Projects

	Project A	Project B	Project C
Expected profit ($)	885,000	705,000	680,000
Breakeven probability (%)	70	72	35
5-percent value at risk ($)	5,800,000	5,840,000	3,930,000

How can the interplay of projects reduce risks?

In the last example we saw that by taking a proactive stance in the face of uncertainty, we could save a lot of potential trouble. Another way to be proactive is to take advantage of the portfolio effect. The first part of the portfolio effect comes from the simple act of diversifying your assets. This is what causes the percentage uncertainty in capitation risk to decrease with the size of the group covered. Another important aspect of the portfolio effect is based on the interplay between the projects in your portfolio.

As an example of the interplay effect, suppose you are the CFO of a healthcare organization. Three potential projects have been presented by management, of which you must choose two. Table 4-3 outlines the projects in terms of expected profit, probability of breaking even, and 5-percent value at risk. Looking at these numbers it seems clear to pick projects A and B. Who in their right mind would go for a project that had only a 35 percent chance of breaking even?

But, it turns out that projects A and B are in the same medium-sized municipality, and one of the major employers in this area may move its headquarters to the city where project C is located. This outcome would have a detrimental effect on projects A and B, but a positive effect on project C. Histograms of the three projects generated through Monte Carlo simulation are shown in Figures 4-11a through 4-11c.

The tallest bars on the right in the histograms for projects A and B reflect the scenario in which the employer stays in town. The bump on the left represents the scenario in which the employer leaves, in which case both projects are likely to lose money.

FIGURE 4-11a. Distribution of Project A

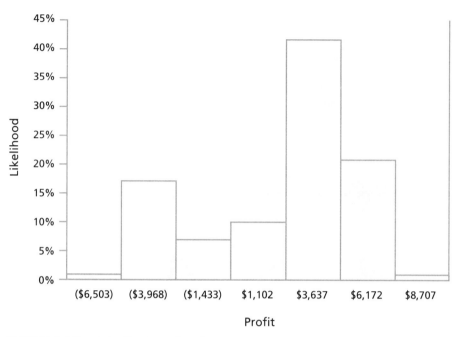

FIGURE 4-11b. Distribution of Project B

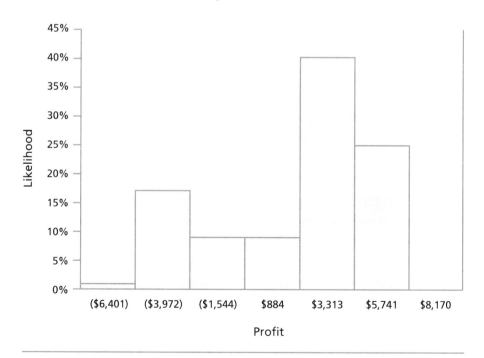

FIGURE 4-11c.   Distribution of Project C

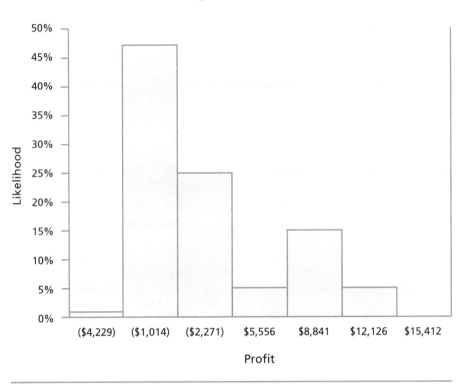

The raised bar on the right in the histogram of project C reflects the case in which the employer leaves town, but for this project the move is a windfall. The tallest bars on the left indicate the more likely scenario that the employer stays.

Now which two projects do you pick? The traditional approach of evaluating the projects individually and then ranking them would lead to rejecting project C out of hand because of its small chance of breaking even and low expected value. The logical choice would seem to be projects A and B, the two with the highest expected profit. Figure 4-12 demonstrates the histogram of this combination generated through simulation. The resulting expected profit is $1,590,000 with a 73 percent chance of breaking even, and a 5-percent value at risk of $12,020,000.

FIGURE 4-12.   Distribution of Portfolio of Projects A and B

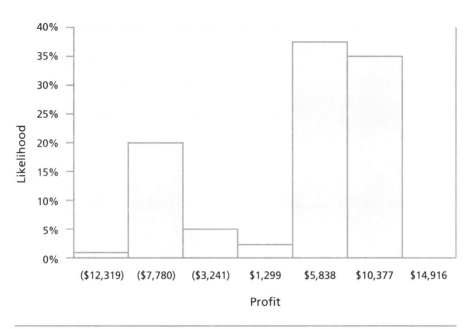

Now let us consider the portfolio consisting of projects A and C. The simulation displays a very different distribution for this combination (Figure 4-13) than it did for A and B.

The expected return of this portfolio is $1,560,000, about 2 percent less than the portfolio consisting of A and B; the probability of breaking even has increased from 73 percent to 77 percent; and the 5-percent value at risk is $2,220,000, less than one-fifth of that for the A plus B portfolio. How was it possible to so drastically cut our risk with just a 2-percent reduction in average profit? Project C formed a natural hedge, or partial insurance against the employer leaving town. The results of all three combinations of two projects out of the three are shown in the Table 4-4.

On its face, Project C looks like a bad investment, but so does fire insurance, until you remember that you also have a house in your portfolio that you want to protect.

TABLE 4-4.   Results of Combinations of Projects

	A and B	A and C	B and C
Expected profit ($)	1,590,000	1,560,000	1,381,000
Breakeven probability (%)	73	77	73
5-percent value at risk ($)	12,020,000	2,220,000	1,910,000

FIGURE 4-13.   Distribution of Portfolio of Projects A and C

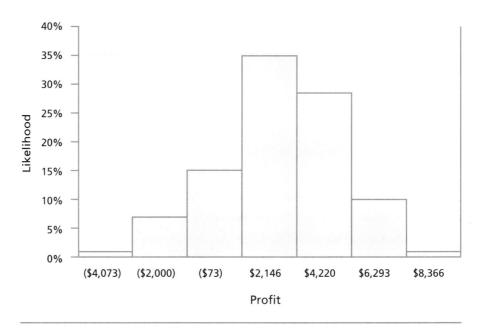

Can we really put this approach into practice?

So you are not convinced. These examples look simplistic, the real world seems much more complicated, and you are just going to keep on plugging averages into business plans. Suppose that instead of urging you to use distributions, I suggested that you look both ways before crossing the street.

SIDEBAR 4-1. Resources

- *INSIGHT.xla*—This is a book and Excel-based software developed to help people get off the ground with Monte Carlo simulation and other analytical techniques (see *www.AnalyCorp.com*).
- @risk and Crystal Ball—Industrial-duty Monte Carlo simulation packages for spreadsheets (see *www.palisade.com* and *www.Decisioneering.com*).
- ENUFF Advisor®—This financial planning decision support software combines the ease and flexibility of a spreadsheet application with reporting and data management features of a database environment (see *www.kaufmanhall.com*).

Would you have responded that because you are crossing a freeway instead of a street, that you would be justified in keeping your blinders on?

This approach is actually quite easy to apply to your own spreadsheet. Sidebar 4-1 lists some resources to help you get started. Remember that even an imprecise modeling of distributions is usually better than a model based on precisely accurate averages. Furthermore, the process of grappling with simulation models will actually make you better at making gut decisions.

References

Hertz, D. B. 1979 (1964). "Risk Analysis in Capital Investment." *Harvard Business Review* 57 (5): 168–80.

Huff, D. 1993 (1954). *How to Lie with Statistics.* New York: W.W. Norton.

Savage, S. L. 1998. INSIGHT.xla *Business Analysis Software for Microsoft Excel.* Pacific Grove, CA: Duxbury Press.

*S*PENDING THE DOUGH: ALLOCATING CAPITAL

IMAGINE TRYING TO play softball without any rules. Three strikes don't make an out, so the neighborhood bully remains at the plate swinging away for hours. When he tires, whoever races to the plate first gets to hit next. Teams do not have a set number of players on the field, so team A has 18 people positioned between center and right field, and team B has only one player covering the whole outfield. Who will win this game? In fact, is this a game worth playing? Without a level playing field, wouldn't and shouldn't one team quit in disgust?

What is capital allocation and why is it important to my healthcare organization?

An organization that has successfully implemented the financial planning process described in Concept Two has assured itself sufficient resources (i.e., capital) to support its strategic objectives. Now comes the equally important task of deciding how to deploy or allocate that capital. *Capital allocation* is the process used to make capital investment decisions. All sophisticated healthcare organizations have strategic and capital investment requirements that significantly exceed available capital capacity. Capital allocation involves determining whether any or all of the many potential capital projects generated during the planning process make sense for the organization. It entails creating a level playing field to separate the wheat from the chaff and keep the players in the game.

Why is capital allocation important? The long-term success of your healthcare organization is highly dependent upon the capital investment decisions made today. Every decision either adds to or reduces the value of the overall operation. The cumulative effect of these incremental decisions determines the organization's future financial success.

Decisions must add to the organization's value—to its ability to raise capital for future projects, maintain or improve its creditworthiness, and accomplish its mission. For every investment that does not generate the expected revenue or value, your organization must seek other ways to obtain the cash flow and capital that should have been generated. Revenue sources are harder and harder to find. In an environment of declining reimbursement, scarce resources, and increased competition, the cost of making bad capital investment decisions is both immediate and severe. The safety net provided in the past era by cost reimbursement and indemnity insurance no longer exists. Credit markets have tightened; the industry's operating cash flow has declined. To survive and succeed in the current environment, your organization's capital allocation process must be based on principles of corporate finance, involving rigorous and consistent application of proven quantitative techniques. This will be further discussed later in the chapter.

Who is responsible for the capital allocation process?

By nature, the capital allocation process involves politics and money. Because the process allocates capital, it also allocates influence and power within the organization. With so much at stake, the process must be led and supported by the CEO. If CEO leadership is not at the forefront, the organization naturally will use more informal, subjective approaches to allocation.

What approaches typically have been used to allocate capital and what can we learn from these?

Many not-for-profit healthcare organizations have historically approached capital allocation on a subjective basis, essentially ignoring quantitative analysis. They assume that their core business can generate sufficient cash flow on an ongoing basis to support investment initiatives that may not have acceptable returns. Many organizations continue to allocate capital subjectively. The department, service, or unit that demands the most gets the most. This is a *political allocation approach.* The problem? Squeaky wheels with newly applied capital grease do not always bring the best returns.

Another approach is to allocate capital according to what was allocated the previous year. Under this type of *historical benchmark approach,* if a hospital's radiology department or one hospital in a multihospital system received $X million or X percent of the total capital dollars in 2000, it would expect to receive the same and maybe even an increased number of dollars or a similar share in 2001. The problem is that in today's turbulent healthcare environment, past performance may be the worst predictor of future results. For example, investing in inpatient services, prevalent in past decades, no longer consistently brings revenue growth or acceptable profitability.

Perhaps the most prevalent approach to capital allocation in healthcare is the *first come–first served approach.* In many organizations, specific projects are evaluated in a serial fashion as they arise throughout the calendar year. The critical problem is that, at the end of the fiscal year, no capital may be left to fund a project capable of bringing significant growth to the organization.

Finally, the *go-with-the-flow approach* to capital allocation involves no methodology and no articulated policy. The organization tries to fund whatever comes along, without the benefit of an evaluative process. The problem here is that not to decide is in fact to decide by default.

What are the characteristics of a healthcare "best practices" capital allocation process?

A "best practices" approach to capital allocation for healthcare organizations should be akin to the approach used by *Fortune* 500 corporations. Key elements of the corporate approach are a sound financial plan; project review and a peer-review approval process; coordinated calendar and planning cycles; and the use of corporate finance–based analytical concepts. Each is described below.

Financial objectives and policies. Capital allocation must be based on sound strategic and financial plans. The strategic plan must include good ideas worthy of investment. If the ideas articulated in the plan will not generate revenue, either go back to the drawing board and think up ideas that will do so, find someone who can, or, if all else fails, get out of the business. A sound financial plan creates the framework to generate required capital capacity. Operating targets outlined in the plan and tied to the long-term strategy specify the amount of cash flow available each year to fund capital investments.

The capital allocation process must have clearly articulated objectives and principles. For example, a multihospital system might include in its written description of the capital allocation process two key principles covering the consolidation of capital available for investment and access to capital. The first principle states that all cash generated by all of the organizations within the system is consolidated and becomes available to meet needs within the system. The second principle states that all organizations within the system have equal access to cash flow generated by system components. Even though a facility may be losing money, it will be offered access to capital for an opportunity that is judged to represent potential for significant return. Such principles must be articulated and agreed upon up front.

Project review and peer-review approval process. The capital allocation process must include a specific, standardized project review process that is used consistently. Standardized formats for each project under consideration help to ensure true comparability. Rational and consistent evaluative guidelines and uniform decision criteria ensure unbiased decision making. A formal batch review process facilitates comparability of the uniform criteria. An organization should approve capital expenditures by establishing a peer-review process that reflects the organization's best strategic thinking.

A coordinated calendar and planning cycle. Effective allocation of capital requires the coordination of the financial planning, budgeting, and allocation processes. Each should be interdependent and rigorously observed so that projects do not slip in and out of the process without appropriate review. All staff should be aware of when capital request project analyses are due.

Figure 5-1 illustrates the integration of the planning, budgeting, allocation, and approval processes. From planning to approval, the cycle takes a full year to complete. Typically, strategic planning takes three months and

FIGURE 5-1. Best Practices Capital Allocation Is Driven via Calendar Management

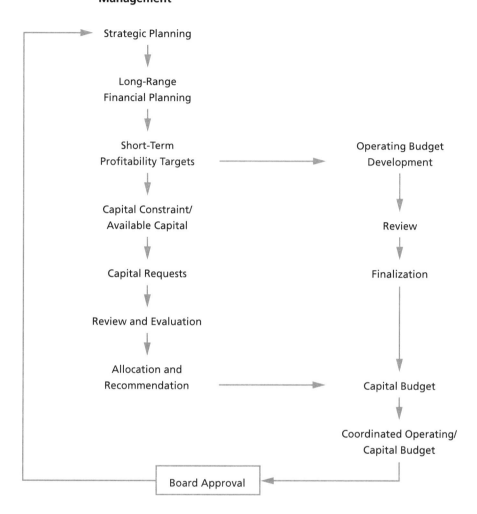

Source: Kaufman, Hall & Associates. Used with permission.

financial planning another two months, leaving budgeting and capital allocation approximately seven months. At the end of the year, the coordinated operating/capital budget is presented for board approval. Those making the presentation describe the organization's five-year strategic plan, the long-term financial plan based on this strategic plan, the operating budget, and allocation recommendations supporting the capital budget. Tying the processes to a firm calendar schedule helps to manage those processes throughout the year. As Figure 5-1 reveals, capital allocation is an integral part of the organization's decision-making cycle.

Corporate finance–based analytical concepts. Effective capital allocation depends on the competent use of quantitative techniques used in corporate finance. These include the net cash available for capital, incremental cash flow projections, discounted cash flow or net present value, and weighted average cost of capital. The mechanics of selected techniques are described later in the chapter. Although capital allocation does involve some qualitative analysis, the use of quantitative techniques ensures a "common language" and outcomes or end points that can be compared for each project under consideration. Qualitative issues can be quantified by building risk assessment into the process (see Concept Four). When push comes to shove, an organization's long-term viability and value comes from its ability to generate a financial return. Each project's return needs to be quantified. A positive return gives the organization the ability to invest in the next strategy. A consensus-driven approach to capital allocation—one focused on what may "feel good" and "look nice"—does not provide the quantitative measures necessary to evaluate financial return. Analytical techniques derived from the principles of corporate finance provide such measures.

Finally, a best practices approach to capital allocation takes into consideration the organization's decision-making style and culture. It must be flexible enough to be adapted as necessary and allow for a multiyear implementation time frame. Most healthcare organizations do not try to tackle the full process during the first year. Implementation over two to three years helps to create buy-in and institutionalization of the approach as part of the organization's decision-making process.

How do we ensure successful implementation of a solid capital allocation process?

The successful implementation of a best practices capital allocation process is dependent on the quality of its design, roll-out, analytical requirements, governance factors, and evolutionary capability. Each of these factors, described in the next sections, must be effectively developed and implemented.

What factors are key to the design of a high-quality capital allocation process?

A good process starts with thoughtful design that melds sometimes disparate ingredients into a cohesive program. Key ingredients include principles of corporate finance, healthcare industry practices and issues, and organizational culture and mission. Analytical tools used in corporate finance will be new to many and need to be taught, particularly to department manager–level staff. It is absolutely critical to ensure that education about tools and techniques is directed beyond the finance department and into line management positions.

A best practices design also addresses the following:

- A contemporary definition of capital. This definition extends beyond the traditional definition of capital as property, plant, and equipment to embrace everything that appears on the cash flow statement. It includes such items as working capital funding for physician losses, joint ventures investments, and all other items that take cash out of the organization.
- Appropriate access to organizational cash flow. This ensures equal footing among all organizational participants.
- Methods for determining the capital constraint. This involves determining the size of the pie. How much can the organization afford to spend on capital investments? Some organizations look simply at net income plus depreciation as a starting point. To this, they need to add all sources and uses of funds, and deduct principal payments, working capital changes and additions to cash. The remaining sum is the net cash available for capital or the capital constraint.
- Evaluation of emergency and out-of-cycle requests. Although batch (nonserial) evaluation of capital requests is key to an effective capital allocation process, the organization should consider how to

build in enough flexibility to accommodate the evaluation of occa-
sional off-cycle requests.

- Appropriate dollar levels for project review. Organizations should establish a threshold for the projects requiring detailed analysis. Not all projects on the table will warrant detailed financial analysis. A first-year threshold should include 50 to 60 percent of total dollars to be spent, perhaps covering 20 to 30 projects. As the organization gets more comfortable with the process, the threshold can be increased to 70 or even 80 percent.
- Integration of project timing with projected organizational cash flows. This seldom gets the attention it deserves. Once your organization establishes a capital budget, staff should review performance from operations each and every quarter, comparing performance to the budget. Organizations must evaluate how they are doing from a cash flow perspective. Is net income plus depreciation less principal payments and working capital better than budgeted? If so, your organization can put dollars back on the balance sheet or allocate them to other projects that did not make the first cut. If performance is worse than budgeted, your organization needs to scale back its capital spending.
- Post-project monitoring. This ensures that cost and revenue projections are on target.

How do we define the capital constraint?

Every organization faces a limit on its capital resources. The limit is determined by its current operations, debt structure, and cash position. To make informed and timely decisions, this limit must be well understood. Organizations that do not understand their capital constraint often waste energy on ideas that have no chance of being implemented.

To define the capital constraint, start by asking the following simple question: What amount of capital are we reasonably sure we can provide to support the organization's development over a defined period of time? This relates to how much the organization can and should borrow and the level of cash that it can generate from operations in uncertain times. Confirm the targets for cash, debt service coverage, and debt-to-capitalization ratios established in the financial plan, and translate these into annual goals. Next, reconfirm the organization's debt capacity based on current-year operations and identify a five-year financial projection scenario to which the organization can commit. To get a complete picture of capital availability, construct a table itemizing sources and uses of capital.

What factors are key to a successful roll-out of a high-quality capital allocation process?

The successful roll-out of a high-quality capital allocation process requires commitment to that process throughout the organization. As mentioned earlier, commitment must originate from the top leaders and pervade all levels of management. A strong knowledge base about the principles of corporate finance and understanding of the capital allocation process by organizational constituencies build commitment.

Comprehensive communication of all aspects of the process is essential to success. Aspects to be communicated include steps in the allocation process, process methodologies, basic corporate finance principles, project-based analysis, and the process calendar. Communication routes must be both broad and deep, including the board of directors, senior management, department directors, and clinicians.

Effective supporting materials are vital as an ongoing reference. A manual describing the process and how to participate offers an effective implementation tool and can also provide basic information on corporate finance principles. The focus of the package should be on middle management as well as senior management. Clinical staff must be educationally empowered to generate ideas, perform the financial analysis, and present their projects in a competitive arena. Decentralization of this process increases its efficiency and effectiveness. Finally, the use of organizational champions to support implementation and provide an ongoing resource can be very successful.

Typical barriers to successful roll-out and strategies to overcome such barriers appear in Figure 5-2.

FIGURE 5-2. Barriers to Successful Roll-out and Strategies to Overcome
             Such Barriers

- *Avoidance:* Expressed as "This process involves too much work," this barrier can be overcome by indicating that the project under consideration represents a significant investment. If the project is not worth the upfront analysis, why is it worth the investment?
- *Misperception:* Expressed as "My project is different," this barrier can be overcome through use of the common language of net present value (NPV). Not all projects will have a positive NPV, but through the objective quantification of financial return, each will be evaluated on an equal footing.
- *Misunderstanding:* Expressed as "This is a defensive project. Its benefits cannot be quantified," this barrier can be overcome by indicating that all projects can be quantified and by quantifying the cost of not investing in the project. Organizations can use a portfolio approach, evaluating whether the portfolio as a whole adds value to the organization.
- *Subversion:* Expressed as "I will just go to the CEO. He or she always approves what I want," this barrier can be overcome by the CEO's use of the formal capital allocation process as a means to say "no." The process forces decisions out of the hallway or private office and into the conference room.

Source: Kaufman, Hall & Associates. Used with permission.

What governance factors are key to the success of a high-quality capital allocation process?

Governance is the linchpin to success of the capital allocation process. Participation of the operational executive team (as discussed earlier) and peer review as an explicit component of project approval are critical to success. Peers know the questions to ask. They can help make the scarcity of resources real for colleagues. In addition, ongoing measurement must be built into process governance. Measurement provides credibility, enabling actual results to be compared to projected results. It helps to ensure that performance can be used accurately as a factor for future capital allocation. Individuals that know that they will be held accountable for performance results typically provide a high-quality analysis up front.

Can and should the capital allocation process evolve and change over time?

The capital allocation process must be capable of evolution and change over time. The process should be reviewed annually to assess its progress toward meeting specified goals. This involves looking at what works and why, what does not work and why, what needs to be added, and what components are unnecessary and can be eliminated. Review of the process, in fact, should be a formal component of the process steps and should occur at approximately the same time each year. Organizations should be willing and able to adjust the process to meet that organization's needs. For example, adjustments may need to be made to the schedule, analytical components, and dollar thresholds. Individuals participating in the process at both the leadership and department levels should be empowered to make necessary changes to enhance the process.

What are the specific goals of project analysis?

The goals for investment or project analysis are four-fold:

1. *To define the scope and intent of the project unambiguously.* Obviously, it is impossible to productively debate the merits of any initiative without substantive agreement on the facts.
2. *To identify the value that the project either adds to or subtracts from the organization.* Financial return need not be the only measure of a project's worth. An organization may decide that it wants to pursue a particular project even if it brings no financial return. However, no project should proceed without the organization's understanding of its value and effect on capital. Every proposed investment,

even a parking garage, must be supported by a comprehensive analysis including projected free cash flows; net present value that takes into account timing, uncertainty, and cost of capital; and cannibalization, which looks at the effect of the project on other projects and operations.

3. *To delineate risk and success factors.* Educated risk taking involves understanding which variables need to be monitored and managed to ensure an initiative's success. Risk simulation looks at what happens if the organization does not go ahead with the project.

4. *To provide a yardstick for review.* Organizations must compare actual outcomes of accepted investments with budgeted results to assess progress and ensure the integrity of its analytic and decision-making process. Project analysis always should include an exit strategy. This involves defining the point at which the plug is pulled on an initiative, upfront and ongoing measurement of the initiative's progress toward meeting concrete goals, and objective post-project decision making to pull the plug if necessary.

What factors should be considered as the first steps of project analysis?

Four factors should be considered as the first steps of analyzing potential capital investments:

1. *The expenditure threshold.* Your organization should establish an expenditure threshold for capital projects that trigger one or more levels of analysis or review. A reasonable relationship should be established between the size and risk of the investment, the level of analysis required, and the level of the organization at which the review takes place.

2. *A project champion.* Once a significant project is beyond the idea stage, it needs a champion who will see it past any hurdles and through to implementation. In many cases, the appropriate champion is the department head or leader who will have line responsibility for the project if it is implemented.

FIGURE 5-3. Business Plan Components

- A project description, specifying facilities, equipment, services, location, and dollars.
- A description of how the proposed initiative fits within the organization's current strategic development philosophy and mission.
- A market assessment sufficient to provide a good sense of the dynamics of the market and its competitors as well as a rationale for volume, service, and revenue projections.
- An implementation plan that delineates key tasks, dates, and challenges of implementation.
- A five-year financial analysis. This includes an income statement, balance sheets, and statements of changes in financial position. Sufficient detail should be supplied for the reader to understand the assumptions underlying the numbers, and the process should highlight the variables critical to the project's success.
- A strategy for modification and termination. This should identify appropriate warning signals and delineate the steps that would be taken to limit the organization's risk.

3. *Definition of the analytic framework.* This involves participation of senior leaders in identifying the key planning issues at hand and the levels of analysis necessary to respond to these issues.
4. *Development of a business plan.* To facilitate informed decision making, a thorough business plan describes the idea and its financial effect in significant detail. It provides the basic documentation necessary for capital decisions. Components of a proper plan appear as Figure 5-3.

What quantitative techniques can be used to analyze a potential investment?

Net present value analysis is the most valuable technique that can be used to analyze a potential investment. At the core of corporate finance, this simple and reliable technique distills the financial ebbs and flows of a project to a single dollar value. Because it does so, it enables evaluation of the project on its own merits and helps to answer the question of how the project might compare financially to others under consideration.

Each project generally requires an initial capital expenditure. This is followed by a start-up period during which financial losses may occur. Then, hopefully, the project enters a period of financial performance that represents a return on the investment.

Net present value is based on two principles: a dollar today is worth more than a dollar next year; and higher risks require higher rewards. The basics of net present value analysis appear in Sidebar 5-1.

What values must be known to perform a net present value analysis?

Four elements must be known to perform a net present value analysis: an estimate of the upfront investment, a forecast of free cash flows, a cost of capital estimate, and a terminal value estimate. Each is described below.

An estimate of the upfront investment should be reasonably clear if a proper business plan has been developed for the project. Be sure to look only at incremental expenditures, ignoring outlays already made. These, in effect, are sunk costs. Do not neglect to include opportunity costs. For example, if the project is a building that is to be built on land that could be sold for a certain price, the value of the land should be considered. Consider also working capital requirements such as operating expenses that will need to be paid from cash reserves before the project is able to carry these expenses on its own.

A forecast of free cash flows involves determining how much cash is generated in a particular year—cash that could be available to distribute to an investor. Free cash flow is equal to net income plus depreciation minus increases in working capital requirements minus capital expenditures. Depreciation and allocation of existing corporate overhead should not be considered in the forecast. In addition, because the cost of capital will be considered separately (see below), projections of free cash flows should assume that the project is financed with equity. Therefore, interest or principal

SIDEBAR 5-1. Calculating Net Present Value

The future value of a present sum of money is expressed as $FV = PV (1+r)^t$ where:

> FV = Future value
> PV = Present value
> r = Interest rate
> t = Number of time periods

By rearranging the above terms, it is possible to express the present value of a future cash flow as follows:

$$PV = \frac{FV}{(1 + r)^t}$$

The present value of an investment decision that results in a series of future cash flows may be expressed as follows:

$$NPV = C_0 + \frac{C_1}{(1 + r)^t} + \frac{C_2}{(1 + r)^2} + \frac{C_n}{(1 + r)^n}$$

where

> NPV = Net present value
> C_0 = Upfront expenditure associated with the investment
> $C_0, C_2...C_n$ = Particular cash flows expected in particular periods
> r = Interest (or discount) rate

As an example, assume that an invesment of $50 now would yield cash flows of $25 per year for three years and that the discount rate is 10 percent. The NPV of that investment would be:

$$(\$50) + \frac{\$25}{1.1} + \frac{\$25}{(1.1)^2} + \frac{\$25}{(1.1)^3} = (\$50) + \$23 + \$21 + \$19 = \$13$$

In corporate finance theory, the decision rule is that the investment is acceptable if has a positive NPV, because this means that the investment generates more than the opportunity cost of capital.

payments should not be included in the projections. Remember to explicitly estimate the effect of incidental factors such as increased market share, incorporate the effects of inflation on revenues and expenses, and include ongoing capital requirements necessary to keep the project going.

The cost of capital involves determining the rate at which the cash flows should be discounted. If the project is risky, it should have a higher expected return than money invested in relatively risk-free investments. How should the discount rate be set to account for the risk of a particular investment? A wide diversity of answers to this question exist in both the business and healthcare communities. A number of methods can be used, but common to all methods is the conclusion that the real cost of capital is significantly higher than the cost of tax-exempt debt. Generally, the weighted average cost of capital is well recognized by investment bankers and financial consultants as an excellent proxy for the cost of capital for not-for-profit organizations. See Sidebar 5-2 for a demonstration of calculating the weighted average cost of capital.

The terminal value of a project is the estimate of the investment's value after the original forecast period. Terminal value can account for 30 to 60 percent of the investment's total value. The calculation can be approached in four ways:

- To assume *no value,* which would be appropriate for an item such as a computer;
- To calculate *liquidation value,* which is the anticipated sale value of the asset on the open market at the end of the projection period;
- To calculate the *annuity/perpetuity value,* which assumes that the investment will continue to generate free cash flow equal to that of the last projection period during a period ranging from one year to forever; and
- To calculate the *growth perpetuity value,* which involves an assump tion about the rate of growth of free cash flow after the projection period.

Remember that the terminal value of the project accrues at the end of the forecast period. The terminal value must be discounted at the same discount rate back to the beginning of the forecast period to define it present value.

SIDEBAR 5-2.   Calculating the Weighted Average Cost of Capital

The weighted average cost of capital (WACC) can be expressed as

WACC = [R(e) x E] + [R(d) x D], where:

  R(e) = Cost of equity capital (see below)
   E = Percentage of equity in capital structure
  R(d) = Cost of debt
   D = Percentage of debt in capital structure

  R(e) = Cost of equity capital can be calculated as
  R(e) = R(f) + B[R(m) – R(f)], where
  R(f) = Risk-free rate (based, for example, on 30-year
      treasury yields)
R(m) – R(f) = Marketwide risk premium
   B = Beta (risk)

For an example health system, the variables are as follows:

  R(e) = 16.05%
   E = 74.00%
  R(d) = 5.00%
   D = 26.00%
  R(f) = 6.449%
R(m) – R(f) = 8.000%
   B = 1.20

Long-term debt is $1,300,000; fund balance is $3,700,000

The cost of equity capital equation, R(e) = R(f) + B[R(m) – R(f)], would read:
16.05% = 6.449% + 1.20[8.000%].

The weighted average cost of capital equation, WACC = [R(e) x E] +
[R(d) x D], would read: 13.18% = [16.05% x 74.00%] + [5.00% x 26.00%).

Note that as the beta or risk factor used in the equation increases, so
does the weighted average cost of capital. Therefore, with a beta of 1.30,
for example, the WACC is 13.77 percent. A beta of 1.50 yields a WACC of
14.95 percent.

How do we select projects?

The traditional way to select projects according to corporate finance theory is to rank them, placing the project with the highest net present value (NPV) first. This is followed with projects of lesser NPV in order of value. According to this approach, all projects with a positive NPV are selected, and those with a negative NPV are discarded.

Some organizations establish a weighting system that captures mission, strategy, and financial issues in a composite ranking. Independent of the weighting system used, however, all truly effective ranking procedures list the projects in a complete table in descending order of NPV. Such a table allows an organization to consider the list as a whole. Does the list have a positive or negative NPV? If the organization selects this list of projects, is the organization adding to or detracting from its value? Clearly, no organization can carry a series of investment decisions that adversely affect its value.

As your understanding of the essential concepts of corporate finance increases, you can begin to combine principles to further focus and sharpen the analysis. For example, ranking projects by NPV has been a staple of corporate-style capital allocation since the 1950s. However, NPV analysis can be made more powerful by integrating the Monte Carlo simulation techniques described by Sam Savage in Concept Four. Using simulation to further analyze projects creates a much more accurate estimate of risk-adjusted value, which statisticians call expected net present value (ENPV).

For example, your hospital is considering the development of a second cardiac catheterization lab. After following the analytic methods suggested in this chapter, the NPV of the project is estimated to be $750,000 based on the expected demand for the lab's services. Using simulation techniques, you can estimate the whole range of possible NPVs based on hundreds or thousands of scenarios involving uncertain demand and other inputs. Although the NPV associated with the average demand was $750,000, this is not necessarily the average or expected NPV as shown in Concept Four. Simulation not only provides a more accurate estimate of the ENPV, but also illuminates potential hidden risks even in projects with high ENPV.

Ranking the portfolio of projects by simulated ENPV may give you an entirely different and more accurate view of the selection decision than that provided by point estimates. However, as discussed in Concept Four, one can go a step further and select the project portfolio along the lines of an optimal stock portfolio, in which case ranking is replaced entirely by a more global approach.

The proper evaluation of projects and their selection for your portfolio may not be an easy process. However, applying principles of corporate finance immeasurably aides the decision-making process. A well-developed and implemented capital allocation process using these principles ensures your organization's future ability to play ball and live its mission.

TOWING THE LINE: STRATEGIC COST MANAGEMENT

Michael E. Rindler

President, The Rindler Group,
Hilton Head Island, South Carolina

WHAT HAPPENS WHEN a modern ship encounters a severe storm at sea? If designed and constructed properly, the ship will be able to ride out even hurricane-force winds in safety. Its engineers have built into the structure the capacity to survive encounters with violent weather, as long as the captain and crew take appropriate action to ensure the survival of their ship. Survival then is dependent both on the ship's design and the people who crew it working in concert. Maritime history is rich with tales of ships lost at sea when either the design was faulty or the captain's leadership inept.

What happens when a healthcare organization encounters bad weather? As with the ship analogy, the ability to survive must be built into the design of the organization. But just as important is appropriate action by the executive leaders and staff, the organization's equivalent of the captain and crew. Effective management of costs ensures the organization's survival even during times of turmoil. If this philosophy is built into the organization's culture and ongoing strategy, the organization can ride out rough weather, just like a well-designed and competently led ship. Quick fixes, such as staff reductions or closure of a hospital wing, might work once or twice. However, if violent weather continues, both the ship and healthcare organization are likely to sink. As with ships, the key to organizational survival is a good design and a capable leader at the helm.

What is strategic cost management and why is it important?

Strategic cost management is a leadership philosophy that enables a healthcare organization to achieve the lowest possible costs consistent with delivering excellent quality care and customer service. It involves a two-step process. First, costs must be reduced to the lowest level consistent with the organization's quality standards. Second, costs must be maintained at this level to achieve ongoing financial goals. The "hows" involved in the process are described more fully later in this chapter.

Successful strategic cost management makes it possible for an organization to create the capital capacity required to reach and maintain a leading edge. As described in Concept Two, capital capacity gives a healthcare organization the ability to purchase the latest equipment or build the most advanced facility for the benefit of patients. Strategic cost management provides access to needed capital to improve clinical quality and services. It also creates the operating profits necessary to ensure that the healthcare organization can attract the best possible physicians and staff and give these individuals the best clinical program resources and supplies to do a superb job caring for patients. In short, when strategic cost management is an ongoing part of an organization's leadership approach, it provides the ability to thrive.

Who is responsible for strategic cost management?

Like quality and service excellence, strategic cost management requires leadership commitment and resolve. To achieve success, the board, administrative leaders, and medical staff must all embrace and practice the concept. In fact, because a strategic cost management philosophy encompasses all aspects of the organization, it should be practiced continuously and at all organizational levels. The creative talents and active input of every manager, physician, and employee must be mobilized. With organization-wide commitment to the strategic cost management process, healthcare organizations can achieve optimal financial performance and create an environment of high-quality care and service excellence.

How does strategic cost management differ from traditional cost reduction efforts?

Strategic cost management is an ongoing approach to managing an organization's resources. Traditional cost reduction efforts, in contrast, generally involve a short-term, project-oriented "quick-fix" approach to cost management. Efforts are deployed when profitability drops, lending covenants are violated, or capital capacity weaknesses prevent investing in updated facilities or needed technology. Organizations using quick-fix approaches begin the cost management process when it is already too late. The underlying assumption of such tactical approaches is that cost management is a project or problem that can be addressed either by focusing internal management on the problem or hiring various kinds of consultants to assist with reduction efforts. Some organizations move from one tactical cost management approach to another in search of a solution to the challenge of managing costs. Unfortunately, success usually eludes them.

Enlightened leadership teams view cost management not as a tactical problem, but as a strategic leadership challenge requiring a strategic approach. In this view, "cost control" becomes "strategic cost management," and an integral part of the organization's day-to-day and long-term operating processes.

How can my organization get started with strategic cost management?

The first step toward developing and implementing strategic cost management is for the leadership team to "make the case" for it—in effect, to establish among board members and organization leaders themselves, and then all other constituencies, the need for an integrated and ongoing approach. The need may be expressed in terms of ensuring long-term survival, pursuing an aggressive growth strategy, improving competitive position, or enhancing creditworthiness for future access to capital, for example.

The next step is to begin the financial planning process described in Concept Two to quantify the organization's future financial needs. This should be a disciplined process that takes into account both future capital and future operating financial needs.

Sound financial projections lead to the next step: establishing a strategic cost management goal that is tied to the operating budget and capital allocation process, described in Concept Five. In times of financial distress, the goal will involve cost reductions. In times of financial health, the goal may involve cost management, or, in some cases, cost reductions. To ensure acceptance of and contribution to the strategic cost management goal, the goal must be both understandable and engaging to the board, physicians, and employees.

At this point, many healthcare organizations hire consultants and delegate to them the task of enumerating cost reduction tactics. This approach usually is not successful. A strategic cost management approach turns to the organization's own "experts"—the managers, physicians, and employees who oversee the care of patients—to identify cost management opportunities. Facilitation and technical assistance from consultants to organize the cost management process is recommended with this approach (more on this later in the chapter).

How can managers, clinicians, and staff best be involved in strategic cost management?

As previously mentioned, strategic cost management is a two-step process. Both steps involve managers, clinicians, and other organization staff. Who better to make the decisions necessary for the first step (reducing costs to the lowest possible levels consistent with quality and service standards) than the managers and physicians who oversee the care of patients? After costs are successfully lowered to optimum levels, managers and clinicians also are the best equipped to perform the second step—meeting the ongoing challenge of continuously evaluating costs to ensure that they remain at optimum levels in light of changing demands. Who better to do this than the individuals involved in providing and managing care and operations?

Strategic cost management task forces are a highly effective way to involve managers, clinicians, and other organization staff. Consulting facilitators should be called in at this point to organize the process of forming teams, shape team agendas, and ensure full team participation. Leaders start by identifying middle management staff that directly control the day-to-day expenses of the organization. This group may range in size from 20 managers in a small hospital to 200 in a large academic medical center. Next, interdisciplinary task forces are formed within each area of middle management to critically evaluate all costs in their respective areas of responsibility. Leaders assign each task force a specific dollar goal that is directly proportional to the costs it controls. The task force's challenge is to generate cost management ideas to meet the goal. Note that individual departments are not assigned goals; rather, the task force team is assigned a collective goal.

In addition to task forces composed of middle managers, the organization's senior management and physician leaders are also organized into task forces. Their challenge is to examine costs under their direct control and to recommend options to reduce such costs.

How do task forces operate?

Strategic cost management task forces generally meet several times a week over a short period of time (such as 60 days) to achieve their assigned goals. During its operating period, each task force issues weekly progress reports to the CEO's office. The CEO communicates regularly to the board, physician leaders, and employees about the progress of the task forces, making the process a truly collaborative organization-wide effort.

During the task force process, consultant facilitators assist managers to challenge themselves constructively about reducing costs, and seek insights from physicians and employees. Facilitators also help task forces establish effective group process guidelines that encourage full participation and consideration of all ideas offered by team members. Skilled facilitators provide managers and physicians with guidance about complex finances and expenses, especially the concept of "green dollar" savings versus "paper" savings (see Sidebar 6-1). Can organizations effectively establish and implement the task force strategic cost management process without consulting facilitators? Probably not. Organizations benefit greatly from the process expertise offered by skilled facilitators.

SIDEBAR 6-1. Which Ideas Represent True Savings?

To truly reduce costs, the dollars saved must be green, or real. Many health-care organizations think they are cutting costs when in fact their cost-cutting actions achieve no green dollar savings. For example, an operating room supervisor proposes reducing costs by cutting the time between cases. Although this idea improves efficiency, it does not actually lower hospital costs. To be considered a green dollar reduction, costs must literally "go away." A successful effort to lower use of clinical or office supplies, for example, saves real dollars that would have been spent on such supplies.

To be effective, task forces evaluate everything in their areas of responsibility. Every staff position, every supply, and every service purchased are carefully scrutinized. Brainstorming about costs reduction opportunities is a key activity. If properly structured and truly interdisciplinary, the task force can be enormously creative in identifying workable cost-reduction strategies. At its very best, brainstorming can be described as practiced reengineering. Task force members also consult frequently with colleagues in their respective areas to gain additional ideas.

How are task force ideas put into practice?

When the task force brainstorming is completed, the organization's senior management and physician leaders objectively review the proposed cost reduction strategies to ensure that the strategies do not compromise quality of care or service. Leaders then develop a strategic cost management plan based on the viable strategies.

As a result of their participation on task forces, managers, physicians, and employees who offered the cost reduction ideas are willing and able to implement them. After costs initially have been reduced by these teams, the entire healthcare organization is well equipped to continue managing costs in the long run. Many healthcare organizations make the task force approach an integral part of the annual budgeting or new programs and services planning processes. Managers and physicians who have successfully participated on task forces are able to realistically project costs for future programs. They also are able to work collaboratively in the ongoing challenge of negotiating the best prices for services, supplies, and capital equipment. And, most important, they are able to continuously consider opportunities to make better use of staffing resources to maintain costs at optimum levels, therefore avoiding the periodic "cost reduction campaigns" that plague healthcare organizations that view costs as a tactical rather than a strategic challenge.

Implementation success is much enhanced through the collaborative task force approach. Through such teamwork, strategic cost management becomes an integral part of a successful organization's culture. It becomes a way of life, not a project with a discrete beginning and end.

What are the barriers to success of strategic cost management?

Numerous barriers to success exist in the practice of strategic cost management. The presence of "sacred cows" is a leading barrier. To be effective, the organization's employees, managers, and physicians must be free to brainstorm about all possibilities to reduce costs. Sacred cows get in the way. If a program is protected by a powerful physician or administrator, strategic cost management will not work. If the CEO indicates that no staff reductions will occur during his or her tenure, strategic cost management will not work. If a board of directors vows never to reduce employee benefits or close an out-of-date facility, strategic cost management will not work.

Another barrier to success is benchmarking. National database benchmarks for staffing levels and other expenses such as supplies and purchased services "do not apply" in the minds of many department managers who view their departments as unique. Strategic cost management is a creative process that should not be bound to a database.

Failure to implement is yet another barrier. Some teams brainstorm effectively and create a great menu of cost reduction strategies. However, they then can fall short of their goals because they fail to implement such strategies. Failure to follow up periodically to ensure that the green dollars are actually reduced is another barrier. For example, costs will not be lower following a reduction in lengths of stay unless staffing and other resources are reduced.

Finally, perhaps the biggest barrier of all is a lack of leadership resolve and commitment to strategic cost management. Strategic cost management can be successful only when the organization's CEO is a full and active participant.

What are the key ingredients for success of strategic cost management?

The key ingredient for success is leadership. As mentioned earlier, leadership creates the case for strategic cost management. Leadership inspires task forces of managers and physicians to create the cost management strategies. Leadership then ensures that the strategies are successfully implemented and that dollar savings are actually achieved.

The use of effective facilitators often is another essential ingredient for success. As mentioned earlier, facilitators can help organize the task force process. They can provide guidance in collaboration and can contribute to the creative process. They can help teach and inspire the organization's constituencies to put forth their best ideas.

What outcomes can be achieved by strategic cost management?

Strategic cost management has many powerful outcomes. Success, however, must be measured over years, not months. Practiced successfully, strategic cost management provides emotional and individual ownership of cost management ideas. It empowers staff and physicians with the sense of accomplishment in achieving financial goals. In addition, strategic cost management creates an inherent commitment to implement cost strategies, since the strategies were created *within* the organization. Finally, strategic cost management enhances the knowledge base of organization leaders and staff. It teaches all individuals involved to be continuously vigilant for ways to reduce green dollars while preserving patient care and customer service excellence.

Capital capacity will likely be the chief issue faced by healthcare organizations in the early decades of the new century. Organizations will be able to attain needed capital capacity and flexibility to withstand inclement weather only through constant attention to costs. All healthcare organizations can thoughtfully and effectively manage and reduce costs, but it takes leadership commitment to ensure that cost management penetrates into the bones of the organization and is part of its ongoing strategy. Some organizations will be able to effectively manage and reduce costs; some will not. Those that do will be successful in the future.

SELECTED BIBLIOGRAPHY

Books/Monographs

Berger, S. 1999. *Fundamentals of Healthcare Financial Management.* New York: McGraw-Hill.

Brealey, R. A., and S. C. Myers. 2000. *Principles of Corporate Finance,* ed 6. Boston: Irwin McGraw-Hill.

Chew, D. H. 1999. *The New Corporate Finance: Where Theory Meets Practice,* ed 2. Boston: Irwin McGraw-Hill.

Cleverley, W. O. 1992. *Essentials of Health Care Finance,* ed 3. Gaithersburg, MD: Aspen Publishers.

Eastaugh, S. R. 1998. *Health Care Finance: Cost, Productivity, & Strategic Design.* Gaithersburg, MD: Aspen Publishers.

Gapenski, L. C. 1996. *Financial Analysis and Decision Making for Healthcare Organizations: A Guide for the Healthcare Professional.* Chicago: Irwin Professional Publishing.

Gapenski, L. C. 1999. *Healthcare Finance: An Introduction to Accounting and Financial Management.* Chicago: Health Administration Press.

Gapenski, L. C. 1996. *Understanding Health Care Financial Management,* ed 2. Chicago: Health Administration Press.

Gilkey, R. (ed.). 1999. *The 21st Century Health Care Leader.* San Francisco: Jossey-Bass.

Ginter, P. 1998. *Strategic Management of Health Care Organizations.* Malden, MA: Blackwell Business.

Goldman, S., and C. Graham (eds.). 1999. *Agility in Health Care: Strategies for Mastering Turbulent Markets.* San Francisco: Jossey-Bass.

Griffith, J. R. 1999. *The Well-Managed Healthcare Organization.* Chicago: Health Administration Press.

Kaufman, K., and M. Hall. 1994. *The Financially Competitive Healthcare Organization.* Chicago: Healthcare Financial Management Association.

Kaufman, K., and M. Hall. 1990. *The Capital Management of Health Care Organizations.* Chicago: Health Administration Press.

Moody's Investors Service. 1999. *Rating Methodology: Moody's Evolving Credit Analysis of U.S. Not-for-Profit Hospitals* [Pamphlet].

Nowicki, M. 1999. *The Financial Management of Hospitals and Healthcare Organizations.* Chicago: Health Administration Press.

Orlikoff, J., and D. Pointer. 1999. *Board Work: Governing Health Care Organizations.* San Francisco: Jossey-Bass.

Prince, T. R. 1998. *Strategic Management for Health Care Entities.* Chicago: American Hospital Association.

Savage, S. L. 1998. *Insight.xla: Business Analysis Software.* Pacific Grove, CA: Duxbury Press.

Savage, S. L. 2000. *The Flaw of Averages. Or Why Everything Is Behind Schedule and Over Budget.* New York: John Wiley & Sons (in press).

Zelman, W. N., M. J. McCue, and A. R. Millikan. 1998. *Financial Management of Health Care Organizations: An Introduction to Fundamental Tools, Concepts, and Applications.* Malden, MA: Blackwell Publishers.

Articles

Arrick, M. D., S. A. Gigante, and M. J. Kaplan. 1999. "Health Care in the U.S.: Financial Pressures Mount for a Rapidly Changing Sector." *Standard & Poor's Credit Week Municipal* [Pamphlet]. October 25, 1999.

Bader, B. 1997. "Worshipping at the Corporate Altar." *Trustee* 50 (9): 20–23.

Bellandi, D. 1999. "Let's Not Make a Deal." *Modern Healthcare* 29 (43): 20.

Bellandi, D. 1999. "Moody's Predicts Gloom for Not-for-Profits." *Modern Healthcare* 29 (40): 56.

Bilchek, G. S. 1999. "Deep and Wide: Health Care Boards Look Beyond Their Communities for New Trustees." *Hospitals & Health Networks* 17 (9): 52–56.

Blecher, M. B. 1997. "Capital: Who's Got It? How to Get It!" *Hospitals & Health Networks* 71: (12): 38–40, 42, 44.

Blecher, M. B. 1998. "When Debt's a Credit." *Hospitals & Health Networks* 72 (12): 48–50.

Bruton, G. D., B. M. Oviatt, and L. K. Kallas-Bruton. 1995. "Strategic Planning in Hospitals: A Review and Proposal." *Health Care Management Review* 20 (3): 16–25.

Clement, J. P., M. J. McCue, R. D. Luke, J. D. Bramble, L. F. Rossiter, Y. A. Ozcan, C. W. Pai. 1997. "Strategic Hospital Alliances: Impact on Financial Performance." *Health Affairs* 16 (6): 193–202.

Cocowitch, V. 1997. "New Thinking for Health Care Leaders." *The Physician Executive* 23 (6): 20–23.

Coile, R. C. 1995. "Assessing Healthcare Market Trends and Capital Needs: 1996–2000." *Healthcare Financial Management* 49 (8): 60–62, 64–65.

Devan, V. R., and M. Williams. 1999. "Measuring Up: Benchmarking Tools Can Enhance Executive Performance. *Trustee* 52 (5): 6–9.

Fine, R. P. 1998. "Applying Risk Management Strategies to Strengthen an IDS's Investment Policy." *Healthcare Financial Management* 52 (11): 35–38, 40.

Gardiner, L. R., S. L. Oswold, and J. S. Jahera. 1996. "Prediction of Hospital Failure: A Post-PPS Analysis." *Hospital & Health Services Administration* 41 (4): 441–57.

Harrison, M. 1999. "Capital News: Take Control of It." *Trustee* 52 (7): 22–23.

Haugh, R. 1999. "The Ratings Slide: Are We Headed for a Capital Crisis?" *Hospitals & Health Networks* 73 (8): 40–43.

Health Care Financial Management. 1995. "Renaissance CFO Emerges in Response to Market Pressures." *Health Care Financial Management* 49 (8): 50–52, 54–56, 58.

Kaufman, K. 1994. "Last Word: 10 Attributes of the Financially Capable Hospital." *Hospitals and Health Networks* 68 (12): 72.

Kaufman, K. 1995. "Last Word: Who Manages … Who Leads?" *Hospitals & Health Networks* 69 (21): 62.

Kaufman, K. 1997. "Managing the Strategic Capital Cycle." *Healthcare Financial Management* 51 (12): 52–55.

Kaufman, K. 1999. "How Much Finance Does a Healthcare Organization Need to Know?" Northfield, IL: Kaufman Hall and Associates.

Larson, L. 1999. "What Every Board Should Know." *Trustee* 52 (4): 4–8.

Moldof, E. P. 1994. "Do-It-Yourself Strategic Planning Provides Map to the Future." *Healthcare Financial Management* 48 (2): 26–31.

Moore, L. M. 1998. "Test Your Financial IQ." *Trustee* 51 (6): 10–13.

Player, S. 1998. "Activity-Based Analyses Lead to Better Decision Making." *Healthcare Financial Management* 52 (8): 66–70.

Serb, C. 1998. "Is Remaking the Hospital Making Money?" *Hospitals & Health Networks* 72 (14): 32–33.

Serb, C. 1998. "Joint Ventures: Money for Mission." *Hospitals & Health Networks* 72 (8): 57–58.

Singhvi, S. 1996. "Using an Affordability Analysis to Budget Capital Expenditures." *Healthcare Financial Management* 50 (6): 70–75.

Solovy, A., and R. Sunseri. 1998. "Leading the Way: 1998 Leadership Survey." *Hospitals & Health Networks* 72 (15 & 16): 30–36.

Tobin, W. C., and L. A. Kryzaniak. 1998. "Using Real Estate-Based Financing to Access Capital." *Healthcare Financial Management* 52 (7): 58–60.

Walker, L.W. 1999. "Governing Board, Know Thyself." *Trustee* 52 (8): 14–19.

Wright, A. P. 1997. "Too Closed for Comfort: Trustees Get a Grip on Excess Capacity." *Trustee* 50 (8): 22–26.

About the Author

Kenneth Kaufman is a founder and the managing partner of Kaufman, Hall & Associates. His experience encompasses virtually all areas of capital advisory and corporate finance services.

Since 1976, Mr. Kaufman has consulted to healthcare organizations throughout the country in the areas of financial and capital planning, joint venture development, financial advisory services, and mergers and acquisitions.

Mr. Kaufman is an important contributor to the healthcare field. Over the past years, he has presented more than 200 educational programs to audiences throughout the United States including seminars sponsored by the American College of Healthcare Executives, American Hospital Association, Healthcare Financial Management Association, and the Governance Institute.

Mr. Kaufman is the coauthor of two books, *The Capital Management of Health Care Organizations* and *The Financially Competitive Healthcare Organization.* In addition, his articles have appeared in such major healthcare publications as *Healthcare Financial Management, Trustee, Modern Healthcare,* and *Hospitals.* Mr. Kaufman holds a master's degree in business administration from the University of Chicago Graduate School of Business with a concentration in hospital administration. Mr. Kaufman is a member of the Board of Directors of the Northwestern Medical Faculty Foundation.